W9-AAK-647

BEAUTY QUEEN

BEAUTY QUEEN

INSIDE THE REIGN OF
AVON'S ANDREA JUNG

DEBORRAH HIMSEL

palgrave
macmillan

First published in 2014 by PALGRAVE MACMILLAN® in the U.S.—
a division of St. Martin's Press LLC, 175 Fifth Avenue, New York, NY 10010.

Where this book is distributed in the UK, Europe and the rest of the world,
this is by Palgrave Macmillan, a division of Macmillan Publishers Limited,
registered in England, company number 785998, of Houndmills, Basingstoke,
Hampshire RG21 6XS.

Palgrave Macmillan is the global academic imprint of the above companies
and has companies and representatives throughout the world.

Palgrave® and Macmillan® are registered trademarks in the United States, the
United Kingdom, Europe and other countries.

ISBN: 978-1-137-27882-1

Library of Congress Cataloging-in-Publication Data

Himsel, Deborrah.
Beauty queen : inside the reign of Avon's Andrea Jung / Deborrah Himsel.
 pages   cm
   ISBN 978-1-137-27882-1 (hardback)
   1. Jung, Andrea, 1959- 2. Avon Products, inc. 3. Cosmetics industry—
Biography. 4. Chief executive officers—United States—Biography.
5. Leadership. I. Title.
HD9970.5.C672J864   2014
338.7'64672092—dc23
[B]
                                                            2013037912

A catalogue record of the book is available from the British Library.

Design by Letra Libre

First edition: April 2014

10 9 8 7 6 5 4 3 2 1

Printed in the United States of America.

Dedicated to Mom and Sal

You may not always see eye to eye, but you are still my "rocks."
Thanks for your love and belief that I can do anything.

CONTENTS

9   What's Gender Got to Do with It?   171

10 Traps: Avoidance and Extrication
    Strategies   189

11 The Leadership To-Do List   211

    Notes   219
    Index   223

ACKNOWLEDGMENTS

Andrea Jung: Although you were not involved at all in the book, thank you for being an inspiration to me and to so many others around the world. I only wish the very best for you in your next chapter.

Susan Kropf: Although you were not involved at all in the book, your persistence, focus, and attention to the critical business drivers were always carried out with grace and elegance.

My Avon friends and colleagues: I could not have written this book without you. Thank you for your passion about the work we did together. Thank you most of all for trusting me to report the story with the integrity that it deserves.

Avon representatives: For continuing to be the heart and soul of the company.

My clients and coachees: I always tell you that I learn as much from you as you do from me.

Paige Wheeler at Folio Literary: You provided great representation and found me the right publisher.

Emily Carleton and her team at Palgrave: I cannot thank you enough for your thoughtful feedback, guidance, and belief in the book.

Eileen Early: For epitomizing the true Avon spirit and culture. You are with the angels now.

Mary Lou Décosterd: For your free sharing of your research, model of women's leadership, and friendship.

Jill: For your friendship and your belief in, and support of, me throughout this project and always.

Peter: For your continued mentorship and, most important, for your nuggets of advice early on in this project.

Ram: Your one sentence of advice set the tone for the book.

Taylor: For your keen financial analysis and insight on the Avon financials.

Helen: For all of your research and Chinese translations.

Jennifer: For answering all my legal and FCPA questions.

Rick: For your background on the China corruption scandal.

My Thunderbird friends and colleagues: For allowing me to learn from you and continue my growth.

Brenda: For always being there when I need you.

Alice: For helping me to find old files that I needed and reminding me of events that I may have forgotten.

Wallace: For helping me to secure some critical interviews.

Bruce: For your collaboration.

My close friends and colleagues, Lesa, Barbara, Kathryn, Lee Ann, and Joe: For your friendship and support.

A senior leader (who wishes to remain anonymous): For providing invaluable information, insight, and mentorship.

KEY MILESTONES DURING ANDREA JUNG'S TENURE

1994 Andrea Jung joins Avon as President, Product Marketing for Avon US.

1998 Andrea promoted to COO under Charlie Perrin.

1999 Andrea appointed CEO of Avon Products, Inc.

2001 Andrea elected chairman of Avon Products, Inc.
      Avon launches retail line, beComing in JC Penny stores.

2003 Avon launches mark., a new line and business targeted to young woman.
      JC Penny and Avon end retail venture.

2005 Announcement of first restructuring

2006 Avon granted first direct-selling license in China.

2008 Internal whistleblower alleges improper payments to the Chinese government which would be a violation of the Foreign Corrupt Practices Act.

2009 Announcement of second restructuring
      Liz Smith (CEO successor) leaves Avon.

2010 Silpada acquisition for $650 million
      Acquisition of Liz Earle, high-end UK skin care company.

2011 Avon announces that it is under an SEC investigation for Foreign Corrupt Practices Act violations.

Announcement that Andrea would step down as CEO upon the hiring of a new CEO (but still retain the chairman title).

Avon celebrates 125th year anniversary with "I Believe" tour.

2012   Announcement that Charles Cramb (Vice Chairman and former CFO) is terminated.

Coty proposes unsolicited takeover bid.

Sheri McCoy appointed as new Avon CEO.

Andrea steps down as Avon chairman.

INTRODUCTION

WHEN I WALKED INTO ANDREA JUNG'S OFFICE AT AVON FOR THE FIRST TIME, I NOTICED TWO things: her model-like beauty and poise and a stunning orchid rising from a pot on her desk, in languid purple glory.

I was there to present a leadership development program that her predecessor, Charlie Perrin, had commissioned. Andrea had only recently assumed the post of CEO, and I thought this project would be a good opportunity to help her align Avon's management team with her agenda. Though I had observed Andrea from afar, my visit to her office was different. When she shook my hand and asked me to have a seat, I felt as if I were in the presence of royalty. In her Chanel suit, signature pearl choker, customized President's Red lipstick, and Manolo Blahnik heels, Andrea radiated charisma. It wasn't just her stylishness, though. Andrea was my age and seemed to epitomize the ideal of having it all that women of my generation aspired to. She was exotically gorgeous, extravagantly intelligent, a wife, and a mother. She was also a CEO of "the Company for Women" and had made it to the top in record time. As the daughter of a feminist and a child of the sixties, I was duly impressed.

As we began our introductory chitchat, I complimented Andrea on her orchid.

"Yes," she said. "Jack Welch sent it when I was named CEO."

I didn't see congratulatory gifts from the president or the pope, but perhaps I missed them.

Early in her tenure as CEO, Andrea was acclaimed as one of the first great leaders of the twenty-first century. Her leadership, charisma, and brilliant branding skills produced accolade after accolade. *Time* magazine named her a "global influential," *Fortune* magazine included her on their list of most powerful women, and Dan Rather of CBS interviewed her. Avon grew and prospered under her leadership, and for a while, it seemed as if she could do no wrong.

But Andrea, like every great leader, was flawed, and eventually those flaws caught up with her, which led to her stepping down as CEO, and then as Chairman of Avon's Board in 2012 amid scandal and falling revenues.

Andrea's career at Avon provides the perfect leadership case study. It offers invaluable lessons about finding the right balance between substance and style, selecting the right talent at the right time, dealing with the nuances of global leadership, managing the special challenges of being a female leader today, and much more. At the same time, her story is a cautionary tale, one that suggests the critical importance of being aware of your weaknesses and how they can sabotage you. As the author of an earlier book, *Leadership Sopranos Style*, I believe in the value of studying a single great, but flawed, leader. The obvious difference between that first book and this one is that Tony Soprano was a fictional leader and Andrea is a real one. More than that, though, I knew and liked Andrea, and I worked closely with her at Avon. At the time, as a senior human resources executive, I could not imagine Andrea or Avon faltering—both seemed invulnerable. But in hindsight, and with many post-Avon years as a leadership consultant under my belt, I see things differently.

Still, the questions linger.

Was Andrea's failure simply a result of longevity—that is, that any leader, no matter how great, is bound to fail if they stay too long?

Did Andrea fail to select, develop, and keep key people in place through hubris or for some other reason?

Was there something fundamentally wrong in the organization—in the supply chain, inventory control, or direct sales model—that would have been difficult for any leader to address?

Did Andrea become ensnared by traps that are all but invisible to stressed leaders dealing with one crisis after the next?

These questions still bother me, and this book is in part an attempt to answer them, though the spectacular rise and fall of an iconic organization is a fascinating story in and of itself.

Founded in 1886 by David McConnell, a door-to-door book salesman in New York, McConnell's goal was to offer women a way to earn money in a supportive, family-like environment that served customers as well as communities. At the center of his vision was the Avon representative, who could support herself or contribute to her family by selling products to friends and acquaintances. For many years, the company grew by leaps and bounds, and the Avon lady became an integral part of US culture. More recently, its direct-selling model has lost much of its effectiveness in the United States but flourishes in developing markets—more than 80 percent of Avon's revenues now come from outside of the United States.

In this book, I investigate why twenty-first century leaders succeed and why they fail, and I will use this story as the framework for this investigation. The book begins with a profile of Andrea's career pre-Avon, then traces her path to the role of CEO, her subsequent success, and her eventual exit. In the first half of the book, I will also extract relevant leadership lessons: I'll analyze what Andrea did right and where she came up short and how that impacted the organization and the people around her.

The second half of the book will place those lessons in a larger context. Based on my work as a consultant as well as through research and interviews, I'll use the Avon story as a jumping off point to discuss timely leadership issues. What does Andrea's time as CEO of Avon tell us about the challenges for women when they are in high-profile leadership roles? What does it tell us about how leaders should interact with strong cultures? What does it tell us about how much leaders should rely on their instincts versus leaning on their people and the data?

To answer these questions, I'll occasionally refer to a specific leader or company and in some instances quote my sources directly. Mostly, however, I'll provide a narrative in both sections that relies more on my narrative voice than on the voices of others. Though I interviewed scores of current and former Avon executives, I refrained from attributing information to them by name. Sometimes this was at their request, but I kept their contributions anonymous because I didn't want the chapters in the first half to read like a business magazine profile. I wanted to tell Andrea's story from an analytical perspective.

Whether you're a young manager just starting your career or a midcareer senior executive, this book offers perceptive lessons. Andrea's uncanny instincts, which led her to Avon and a CEO position at a relatively young age, certainly illustrate how to hit the ground running—and how to sustain that pace until you secure a capstone position. Her brilliance at managing her board of directors—they were convinced she walked on water—provides insight into the CEO-board relationship.

This is also a book for women in business. Avon is known as "the Company for Women," but until Andrea arrived, it was run exclusively by men. Her ability to overcome the biases of a male-dominated management team, to inspire other women, and to have it all (a glamorous social life and loving family) were an inspiration. Yet it was also, in some sense, a lonely life. Like some other powerful women leaders, Andrea maintained a certain aloofness. Despite being a friendly, caring person, Andrea would allow people to get only so close. I remember that Andrea once asked another female colleague if she was able to balance both personal and professional relationships at work and was a bit surprised when her colleague answered in the affirmative. "What do you talk about?" Andrea asked her. Sometimes women leaders can err on the side of being too professional—they fail to establish the close, personal work relationships where people let their guard down and tell you what you need to hear.

I should also point out that what I'll be writing about is extremely timely. More so than ever before, leaders are confronting the issues that Andrea confronted at Avon: transitioning organizations to new business models, pursuing global growth strategies, making ethics-versus-profits choices, changing from traditional to technological channels of distribution. These are huge challenges, and Andrea's skill in meeting many of them—and her failure to deal with a critical few—are equally illuminating.

This book is neither an ode to nor an indictment of Andrea Jung. Though I have tremendous admiration for her accomplishments, I am also keenly aware of her faults. So don't expect a puff piece or muck-raking. I'm writing this book first and foremost to foster understanding and learning. I also believe the Andrea/Avon story makes fascinating reading, and so I hope to present this narrative in a way that will keep you turning the pages. At the same time, I believe this story is instructive in the best sense of that term. You'll find a number of how-tos, questions, and other tools derived from Andrea's story, my time with the company, and my consulting experiences.

However, the book will keep looping back to Andrea. Like Steve Jobs, Jack Welch, and other charismatic leaders, Andrea is a great subject. Everyone has a story about her, and so, as much as anything else, this is a book of stories. It is fitting, therefore, that I conclude this introduction with a quick anecdote that captures Andrea in all her paradoxical glory.

Margaret,* an Avon executive, was inspired by Andrea and thought her to be a brilliant CEO and assumed that they had a strong relationship. She made this assumption despite Andrea's inconsistent

---

* Margaret is a pseudonym.

relationship behaviors. For instance, one day she might engage you in meaningful and insightful conversation about your children, the next she would look right past you in the elevator as if you were a stranger. Still, Margaret simply figured this was Andrea being Andrea—she accepted these inconsistencies as a small price to pay for working under a charismatic, brilliant CEO who valued her as a person and as a professional.

One day Andrea asked Margaret to come to her office. This wasn't an unusual request, and Margaret entered the office smiling warmly at Andrea, happy to have an opportunity to have some one-on-one time with her. Margaret walked up to Andrea and gave her a hug and a kiss on the cheek.

Andrea didn't reciprocate either gesture. In fact, the expression on Andrea's face was dismissive—she was communicating with her eyes what she was about to communicate in words. Margaret didn't have a clue that Andrea was about to fire her. In most organizations, executives who work closely with the CEO generally learn to read them well. But Andrea was a private person in a public position. For her, firing Margaret must have been extremely difficult—she hated to make other people upset or unhappy. But rather than offer words of consolation or explanation or soften the blow in any way, Andrea just told her that she was being let go. Margaret was shocked, but she shouldn't have been.

That was the thing about Andrea. As much as you might have thought you knew her, you didn't really. Now, with the advantage of time and distance (and a lot of interviewing), we're about to get to know her much better.

PART ONE

THE AVON STORY

ONE

FASTEST ON THE FAST TRACK

ARE GREAT LEADERS BORN OR MADE? DO THEY CREATE THEIR OWN SUCCESS, OR IS IT THE result of luck and circumstance—of being in the right place at the right time?

Andrea Jung's upbringing and her early career suggest that, if greatness can't be predicted, hindsight can certainly help us trace its emergence. Like many great CEOs, Andrea didn't aspire to the title early on—in fact, she demonstrated little interest in the business world. Yet also like many great CEOs, Andrea was open to and ready for opportunities, and when one arrived, she seized it and didn't look back.

The best leaders tend to find their paths through an odd combination of trial and error and preparation. They are often more likely than the average person to welcome different experiences, and through this trial period they discover a job or field that seems made for them. From that point on, they step onto the fast track and accelerate to the top of companies with blinding speed. As we'll see, this is exactly what happened to Andrea—or, to use the more accurate active voice, it's what Andrea made happen.

In this chapter, I will describe how this daughter of Chinese immigrants became Avon's head of marketing. I'm not going to become enmeshed in biographical minutia but instead I'll give you the highlights of this time in Andrea's life and focus on the circumstances and decisions that turned her from an Ivy League English major into a fashion industry executive.

A BOX OF COLORED PENCILS

The paths to leadership are varied. Many start with cultural heritage or inspiring teachers and role models. Some CEOs talk about how hardscrabble childhoods and poverty motivated them to rise to the top. Others come from privileged backgrounds where leadership is a family tradition.

Among all these backgrounds, one commonality is supportive parents with high expectations, and Andrea's is no exception. Andrea always spoke proudly about being the daughter of Chinese immigrants. She was born in Canada, and her family moved to Boston when she was ten—her father, an architect from Hong Kong, was offered a teaching position at the Massachusetts Institute of Technology (MIT). Her mother was the first woman to graduate in chemical engineering from the University of Toronto. She later pursued music and became a full-time pianist. Whether Andrea's mother or father could be classified as "tiger mothers" is difficult to know, but they both expected her to excel—ideally in law school or medical school.

Though Andrea grew up in a traditional Chinese household in one sense, her mother and grandmother were forward thinking, maintaining that girls can do anything boys can do.[1] Andrea says that she learned perseverance from her mother, who was her role model as both a highly regarded professional and a parent. Her mother had it all, so Andrea aspired to do the same. Andrea also valued her father's patience and learned from him how to remain calm on the outside even when she was feeling anxious. Her family instilled in her a sense of discipline—she studied Mandarin on Saturday mornings, took piano lessons for years, and mastered conversational French—that was later evident in her performance as CEO.

When Andrea was in the fourth grade, she wanted her mother to buy her a box of colored pencils, but her mother told her she must first receive perfect marks in school. Andrea met the objective and received her reward. Early on, she learned the lesson that hard work helps achieve desired outcomes. It is not difficult to see why Andrea became a leader who prized effort and excellence.

These same stories also help explain Andrea's derailment. Dr. Robert Hogan, a well-known psychologist, created an assessment tool years ago that identified leadership derailers—personality traits that emerge under stress when we lose our ability to regulate our behavior. Unaddressed, these actions can sabotage relationships as well as careers. Subsequently, Drs. David Dotlich and Peter Cairo, equally well-known leadership development consultants, wrote extensively about these leadership derailers based on their work with CEOs and other senior executives. The derailers include arrogance, melodrama, volatility, and others. Each derailer has a foundation in our strengths and therefore has a positive flip side—arrogance's flip side, for example, is self-confidence and pride—and these qualities can motivate leaders to deliver outstanding results. Under stress, however, this self-confidence can morph into arrogance. This derailed individual is so convinced of the correctness of his opinion that he ends up alienating colleagues by refusing to take any opposing view into consideration.

One of Andrea's major derailers was being a pleaser; she avoided conflict and tried to appease others in order to maintain harmony, a tendency that can be traced back to the messages she received growing up. Andrea spoke often about how there were no disagreements in her house, especially at the dinner table, because disagreements weren't tolerated. She embraced that heritage, complete with its ideal of the respectful Chinese daughter, yet she was also conscious of its limitations. Her father even warned her that her upbringing might prove a handicap if she chose a career in business, with its cutthroat culture.[2]

Andrea has been very open about her background and its influence on her: "Being a Chinese woman has required some real life reflection on how to lead; the cultural aspects of being Chinese in terms of aggressiveness and being conflict averse."[3] Andrea wanted to please her parents and her teachers, and she was a dutiful daughter and superior student. As a leader, Andrea could make people feel special, and it helped create extraordinary loyalty and performance. Yet her tendency to avoid being the bad guy would be a recurring problem in her career.

In school, Andrea didn't have business aspirations. She was, however, interested in one aspect of school that compelled many top business executives: student politics. As class secretary and then student body president, Andrea already knew how to attract people to her and charm them into voting for her. An excellent student, Andrea finished high school early and entered Princeton. Though her parents hoped that she might become a doctor or a lawyer, Andrea studied English literature and aspired to join the Peace Corps or become a journalist when she graduated magna cum laude.

Fate, however, intervened. College friends suggested that Andrea might want to consider applying for Bloomingdale's management training program before joining the Peace Corps or going back to school. While no one in her family had worked in retailing, her parents thought getting a job—any decent job—would be a good thing for her. It made sense to Andrea; she felt as if she needed toughening up and that this training program would do the trick. Her intention was to stay for only two years. Within two months of starting the program, she was ready to quit. She had been assigned a menial job in the stockroom, removing clothes from vendor hangers and putting them on Bloomingdale's hangers. It was excruciatingly boring, and she told her parents she had had enough. They told her, "You just started! That's not perseverance. We didn't raise you to quit. We don't quit in this family. You have to start your way at the bottom and work your way up. You haven't given it a chance."[4]

Leaders differ wildly in terms of personality and strategy, but the vast majority possess a remarkable stick-to-itiveness that allows them to persist when others would give up. In every leader's career, there will be major obstacles and tough times. Staying the course isn't easy in a fast-changing world where it's tempting to hedge one's bets or quit the game altogether, but Andrea learned a valuable early lesson about perseverance, and it stuck with her.

FINDING A CALLING AND A MENTOR

It was fortunate Andrea stayed at Bloomingdale's, because two events took place during her time there that had a profound impact on her career. First, she became passionately proficient. What I'm suggesting by that term is that not only did she become skilled at and knowledgeable about the fashion business, but she also developed a love for it. Andrea always liked variety and action and not having to stay with one task for too long; the changing trends and cycles of retail satisfied those requirements. She discovered how energizing it was to market to consumers, and she found she had an aptitude for it. This combination of passion and proficiency often provides a career spark, giving budding leaders the confidence they need to take risks and accept stretch assignments that might daunt others.

At Bloomingdale's, Andrea and her merchandisers creatively combined demographics and psychology, linking certain fabrics and colors to evoke memories of childhood. Andrea possessed a unique capability to connect dots, spotting trends early, listening to unmet customer needs, and then being able to see marketable linkages that others missed. She also was not afraid to experiment or try something new. Years later she said of her approach, "You have to combine instinct with good business acumen. You just can't be creative, and you just can't be analytical."[5] For Andrea, the intersection of the two was where the magic happened.

Second, Andrea found her first mentor, Barbara Bass. Barbara was the first woman to head a division of Federated Department Stores, the parent organization of Bloomingdale's. She then became executive vice president and general merchandise manager at Bloomingdale's.

Barbara went on to I. Magnin, the now-defunct California department store, in 1987, and was named its first female Chairman and CEO at age 36. As one of Bloomingdale's first female vice presidents, Barbara was a model for what Andrea aspired to be. She was tough and aggressive but also compassionate. Early on, she worked with Andrea to help her become more assertive—a struggle for Andrea given her inclination to keep things harmonious.

The best mentors not only assist and advise but also help people visualize what they might become in 10 or 20 or 30 years. As Andrea said about mentoring, "Some people just wait for someone to take them under their wing. I've always advised that they shouldn't wait. They should find someone's wing to grab onto."[6] Barbara wasn't a mentor to just Andrea but to many female retail leaders such as Wendy Svarre who made the rounds from Bloomingdale's to Chanel and Armani.

Barbara suggested to Andrea that marketing was a great career path for women in their field, given that women made the majority of the purchasing decisions. She believed that the capstone position of chief merchandising officer of a company like Bloomingdale's should, or at least could, be in the hands of a woman.

Looking back, Andrea was keenly aware of how much she learned from Barbara: "She was instrumental in giving me confidence in how to manage through a situation, not only as a young leader, but as a female leader."[7] To illustrate the value of Barbara's mentorship, Andrea said, "A male executive told me I should be pleased if I was making my age—for example, earning $23,000 per year if I was 23 years old, although it was less than what males were making in the job. When you're young and have a rising career, people assume you can wait. . . . Barbara was a real fighter for me. I learned from her that being a woman and being young are both irrelevant."[8]

While at Bloomingdale's, Andrea also had her first experience managing people, as she became one of the company's youngest vice presidents at age 25, heading up a department with staff that were much older than her. She knew she needed to be more assertive and make the tough calls. She also learned an early lesson about getting work done through others. She recalled, "No longer was I just an individual contributor. I had to be a leader now. What I did was irrelevant. It was all about what people did underneath me. There were personnel changes that had to be made and a new strategy to be designed. The principles I followed were to have a tremendous amount of compassion and respect for people along the way and to understand and value the human spirit along with the work."[9]

From Bloomingdale's, Andrea joined the department store chain J. W. Robinson's but stayed only briefly. Barbara had moved on to a top position at I. Magnin, and she brought Andrea on board at age 28 as senior vice president and general merchandising manager. Though she only stayed for about a year, it was an eventful one. Both she and Barbara faced the challenge of making Magnin's more hip for younger customers—a challenge that would arise again at Avon. During this time, Andrea had her first child, Lauren (though she divorced shortly thereafter). Personally and professionally, Andrea's life was moving quickly. In 1989 she accepted an offer to become Neiman Marcus' executive vice president of merchandising/women's apparel. Neiman's was also looking to attract a younger, more upscale customer as well as continuing their expansion outside the Dallas area. Neiman Marcus was the big time, and it provided her an opportunity to continue to hone her craft and take on increased responsibilities.

Early on, Andrea showed a flair for spotting and capitalizing on fashion trends and getting inside the European runway show scene. It wasn't long before Andrea was hanging out with designer Donna Karan and then-Vogue editor Anne Sutherland Fuchs. Though she was still young and slightly inexperienced, she had already developed her signature style. She wore exquisite designer clothes and projected an air of confidence and marketing insight well beyond her years. People were drawn to her beauty, taste, and bold ideas. In the retail circles in which Andrea traveled, she stuck out. One retailer who knew her then said, "She doesn't put her pants on the same way we do." Another commented, "She is a different breed and at a different level." Even then, she had an aura about her. But she wasn't egotistical or bullying like a lot of other smart and stylish leaders—she was clearly different. Even then, people noticed her when she walked into a room. It wasn't any one thing, but a combination of beauty and brains, of confidence and flair. Most young people in business haven't developed the polish that Andrea possessed seemingly from the moment she stepped in the door.

Part of this difference was that at this point in her career, she was often one of the few women—or the only woman—in the room. Yet unlike some of her female contemporaries, she was not deferential. She had learned how to speak up from Barbara, and she made herself heard. Her presence was palpable not only when she spoke but even when she just sat and listened. It was impossible to dismiss her. It was impossible not to be impressed by her.

There's a reason certain people become CEOs and others do not. The ones who do are restless, even in success. Unlike other executives who have great jobs and do well at them, these positions aren't sufficient to satisfy their ambitions. They want greater challenges. Andrea was already becoming restless, despite her achievements at Neiman Marcus. She was tired of marketing only to wealthy women. She wanted to do something that had meaning and purpose. In 1993 she married Bloomingdale's CEO Michael Gould and moved to New York. They adopted a son, and her daughter from her previous marriage lived with them. Andrea and Michael became a fixture in the New York City social scene at both fund-raisers and other philanthropic events. Still, Andrea was not one to bask in reflected glory; being the wife of a CEO was not her goal.

It was at this crucial moment that a company named Avon came calling.

EARLY CAREER LEADERSHIP LESSONS

1. *Foster recognition of weaknesses and the need to maintain strengths.* As we'll see, Andrea did a much better job of heeding this lesson early in her career than she did in its latter stages. Still, she developed a thick skin when she took the training position at Bloomingdale's and stayed despite the humbling, mundane nature of the job. Similarly, she recognized that she needed to be more assertive and studied leaders such as Barbara Bass to learn how to stand up for what she believed in. At the same time, Andrea recognized that she was good with people and understood that she needed to maintain this ability even as she became tougher and more assertive. Her compassion, especially, was something that she endeavored to integrate into her management style. This was partly a result of Andrea's natural desire to learn and achieve, but she was also fortunate to work for organizations that encouraged well-rounded development. From an organizational standpoint, this means committing to formal and informal methods of assessment and training—mentorship, feedback, and so on.

2. *Value young leaders who are conscious of who they are, how they've been raised, and how it impacts their management/leadership personas.* Some young people believe the only way they can become leaders is by shucking off who they have been raised to be and adopting specific new traits (i.e., decisiveness, impassiveness, etc.). In fact, authenticity is crucial to leadership greatness, and Andrea came off as authentic because she valued who she was and how she had been raised. She readily admitted that she needed to change some of her behavior, but she would never change who she was. Her parents had taught her to be tolerant and respectful of others, a force for

harmony rather than dissonance. She never lost this quality nor tried to hide or deny it. This helped Andrea develop a persona that was both distinctive and genuine.

3. *Provide mentorship opportunities and incentives.* You're never too young for a mentor—Andrea found her first one in Barbara Bass. No matter how smart or skilled, everyone needs at least one person to provide guidance in the early stages of a career if they want to reach the top later on. Bosses are fine, but they may possess neither the time nor the inclination to mentor people—to invest themselves in others' development. At Bloomingdale's, Andrea began developing a sense of the leader she wanted to be and was deliberate about choosing a mentor both who could serve as a role model and who possessed the leadership qualities she lacked. (Recall her mantra, "Find someone's wing to grab onto.") Andrea's father taught her that humility was a part of her heritage. If others paid her a compliment or recognized a strength, her parents would say, "No, no, no. She's not that good." Arrogance was forbidden. Consequently, Andrea was adroit at asking for feedback, seeking out mentors, and gleaning what she could from other great leaders. She was eager to learn, and that receptivity attracted good teachers. Andrea recounted a story about a boss who had a poster on his wall with a picture of a potted plant and the saying, "Bloom Where You Are Planted." Whenever one of his staff would come in and complain about wanting to move to another department or about a peer's behavior, he would point to the poster.[10] What this taught her was that you can learn anywhere and from whomever is willing to help. Again, this receptivity to learning acted as a mentor magnet.

   Later in her career, Andrea was asked to join the board of General Electric, and Jack Welch became another mentor.

Andrea never went on to get her MBA because she often remarked that Welch's tutelage was the best schooling she could have received. Early on in her Avon career, she also took advantage of mentoring by Avon Board member and Time Inc. CEO Ann Moore and retired Rubbermaid and Goodyear Tire and Rubber Company Chairman and CEO Stanley Gault.

Organizations should also encourage their veteran leaders to seek out mentees. Obviously, some leaders are better at this than others, but companies need to reinforce the message that mentorship is valued. Formal mentorship programs are great, but informal mentorship at all levels is even more important. Embedding the concepts of teaching and learning into the culture will help make mentorship more of an organizational reflex than merely a program.

4. *Let people develop personal brands.* This is another way of suggesting that organizations should endorse authenticity. Too often, young leaders feel as if they have to fit a particular company style, that they have to act a certain way to get ahead in an organization. This results in a stultifying sameness. Instead, high potentials should be free and encouraged to develop a singular style that represents who they are. Throughout her career, Andrea was known for her marketing prowess. Even before the concept of personal branding became hot, Andrea anticipated it. She saw in Barbara Bass a powerful but attractive woman who was still able to be feminine. Ask 25 people who know Andrea or are at least familiar with her, and they will tell you she was beautiful, smart, always perfectly groomed, polite, loved designer suits and shoes, never was without her signature pearl choker, and often wore pearl earrings and President's Red Avon lipstick. What she became

known for in her career, though, was her acumen about the women's market and her ability to attract a younger, hip consumer. She also developed a reputation for advocating on behalf of women. She was always very careful to maintain that brand, even in the last difficult years of her Avon tenure.

5. *Give future leaders high-visibility, challenging projects and monitor how they execute them.* At the time Andrea joined the more senior ranks of female leaders, many women felt as though they needed to be twice as good as their male counterparts and do some of the projects that no one else wanted to do to be taken as seriously. In these early years, Andrea was often not just the first or only woman but also the youngest. She used her creativity and unique viewpoint to tackle these high-visibility projects.

6. *Keep an eye out for passion and perseverance.* These two qualities characterize great leaders, and these people usually acquire and display them early on. Andrea's passion for Avon and marketing the brand was part of her aura, and her all-in commitment to what she believed in made that aura burn brighter. I suspect that when Andrea was in the Bloomingdale's training program and succeeded with her initiative to link certain fabrics to memories of childhood, you could see the brightening glow of a leader being born.

7. *Identify derailers.* The sooner young leaders spot them, the better off they and their organizations will be. How do you identify a derailer? Coaching and feedback are key tools; people are often blind to the traits that can cause them to make mistakes because they're the flip side of their strengths. For instance, Andrea's derailers were being aloof and a pleaser, and to a certain extent, she was aware of both tendencies and worked to counteract them. But it's a tricky proposition,

because derailers exert a powerful hold over our behaviors, especially under stress. Andrea was a strong people person who treated her direct reports and colleagues with greater respect and consideration than most businesspeople do—she wanted people to like her, but the danger (and derailer) was that she tried to please them too much. At times she was successful at managing this pleasing derailer, but often it was a struggle that she lost.

TWO

A COMPANY WITH A MISSION, A WOMAN WITH A VISION

WHEN YOU THINK OF GREAT BUSINESS LEADERS, IT CAN BE DIFFICULT TO IMAGINE THEM achieving their success at companies other than the ones that made them famous. Apple's Steve Jobs, Chrysler's Lee Iacocca, and GE's Jack Welch are all deeply identified with their organizations. They found the perfect leadership situations—business challenges that they were ideally equipped to deal with, business cultures that suited their personal styles. Surely they could have done well elsewhere, but would they have achieved greatness?

Obviously, this is an impossible question to answer, but it's worth thinking about in the context of Andrea Jung's arrival at Avon. Avon needed her as much as she needed Avon, and though both sides recognized it was a good fit, they didn't realize it was an ideal fit. Only with hindsight do we gain the perspective that leaders who achieve extraordinary results are usually in positions tailored to their personalities, skills, and strengths.

Let's look at how and why Andrea joined Avon and how circumstance combined with her perspicacity to place her on an ideal leadership track.

MANY LEVELS OF ATTRACTION

As much as Andrea loved a marketing challenge, this was not the only reason she left Neiman Marcus for Avon. Part of her decision to join Avon was related to her husband, Michael Gould, CEO of Bloomingdale's in New York City—she needed a job in New York. But I think Andrea's motivation was deeper. Something about Avon resonated for Andrea. It was a company with the mission of empowering women to be not only beautiful but successful. This struck a chord with Andrea, much as Apple's, Chrysler's, and GE's missions must have struck chords with Jobs, Iacocca, and Welch. On some level, leaders on the cusp of greatness sense when a company's mission matches their personal vision. Part of the decision to join such an organization is analytic, but part, no doubt, is intuitive.

Of course, it's not enough to sense the opportunity if the organization doesn't believe you're the right person for the job. In 1993, Avon's CEO, Jim Preston, wasn't looking for his own replacement, but he was intrigued by a call he received from a recruiting/consulting firm that had worked with Avon in the past. The executive from the firm told Preston that they had recently met with a young woman who was as smart as she was beautiful and was one of the best talents he had ever encountered. He suggested that she had CEO potential.

Preston was impressed by this description of Andrea, and he was keenly aware that Avon needed a catalyst—someone from the outside who could jump-start the company. At the time, Avon was struggling with declining sales, a decreasing number of representatives, and perhaps most alarmingly, a commissioned study indicating that the Avon brand was viewed as your "mother's or grandmother's brand" by the target audience. These results called into question the effectiveness of Avon's traditional direct-selling policy and sparked a discussion of moving products into retail distribution.

This direct sales channel was of great concern to Preston and other members of the management team. The study made it clear that in the United States, the method was perceived as old-fashioned—a perception that seemed to be spilling over onto the brand itself. But he knew that direct selling was alive and well in other countries that lacked strong infrastructures. When people can't go to the local store to pick up brand-name cosmetics, a visit from an Avon representative means something.

Still, with revenues down, Preston was at least considering department store selling options, and Andrea's extensive and successful retail background impressed him. When they sat down to talk, he was even more impressed. Andrea was impressed as well, especially with a small, framed picture that Preston kept behind his desk. Recalling that moment, Andrea said, "The title of the picture was the evolution of leadership. It had four footprints: the first was a footprint of an ape, the second was a bare foot of a man, the third footprint was of a man's wing-tipped shoe. The fourth footprint was a woman's high heeled pump." Andrea asked Jim if he truly believed this. He replied, "We haven't done as good a job on this as we should, but I imagine one day a woman will run this company."[1]

Preston offered Andrea a consulting project: to develop a recommendation about the feasibility of moving toward a more retail-oriented system. What impressed Preston most was how decisively and quickly Andrea handled the project. Andrea suggested that Avon could best compete with department stores by staying out of them; she proposed that Avon needed to upgrade its image with better products and packaging. This would provide the competitive edge the company needed. She was elegant in her delivery and held nothing back. Andrea spoke not as if she were interviewing for a job, but like someone who already had it. And, of course, her ideas benefited from her perspective as an image-conscious woman.

Preston realized that the era of men in suits running Avon was passing, and he hired Andrea to head their US marketing efforts, reporting to Christina Gold, at that time the head of the North American business. Andrea's mission was to contemporize the beauty brands, beginning with packaging. Former human resources staff remembered that they were very excited to have someone of her caliber on board.

There were two other senior women at the time who were seen as potential candidates for the top job. Christina Gold, Andrea's boss, had been brought over from Avon's Canadian group to be the first female head of the North American Group. Susan Kropf, then-president of new and emerging markets (she had started as an Avon secretary) was turning in stellar performances in every job to which she was assigned. Both Susan and Christina had begun their careers at Avon in 1970. And Joe Ferreira, head of Avon's Asia Pacific region, where business was booming, was also a rising star.

So Andrea's path to the top wasn't clear. In fact, at that time she really didn't aspire to be CEO. Her bigger concern at the time was, she said, "that the company had no global marketing agenda."[2] Like many potential CEO candidates, she would have to distinguish herself. CEOs generally aren't chosen because of their consistency, loyalty, seniority, and solid performance. They need to take a risk, develop a compelling persona, and gather sufficient momentum to ensure that, no matter how talented or accomplished their cohorts might be, they are the ones who seem destined for the job.

Andrea met these objectives faster than most but not before overcoming one major obstacle.

THE OUTSIDER BECOMES AN INSIDER

Some corporate cultures are highly insular, and Avon fit that bill. Direct-selling companies are considered different from traditional retailers—not only by those in other types of organizations but by the direct sellers themselves. No doubt, Avon people were skeptical that people coming from non-direct-selling companies really understood their business; some may also have felt that executives from the likes of Bloomingdale's and Neiman Marcus looked down their noses at companies like Avon.

Andrea's work background, distinctive style, beauty, and youth all conspired to label her as an outsider. No one quite knew what to make of her in her initial months at the company. No doubt, people were impressed by the clarity and passion with which she voiced her ideas, and at least some of the people there recognized that her innovative, risk-taking perspective was just what Avon needed to rebound and grow.

At the same time, she didn't look, act, or strategize like a typical Avon executive—the stiletto heels and Chanel suits alone were enough to make people scratch their heads. Could the typical "Avon lady" or even the typical Avon employee relate to someone so un-Avon-like? When Andrea first began working at Avon, the tradition was that new staff spent time in the field to better understand the direct-selling experience. Andrea met with representatives and even worked as one for a short time. Although she said that she was not very good at the job, she was able to see firsthand the customers' difficulty navigating the onerous 125-page Avon brochures that she had just approved.

Perhaps of even greater concern was the question that surrounds every charismatic young leader:

Was she truly committed to the company, or was her primary concern her own glorification?

Andrea's style certainly raised suspicions at the beginning of her Avon tenure. More than one employee at the time noted that they would meet with Andrea and feel that they connected, that she really liked and cared about them. Then, the next day, they would get in an elevator with her, and she wouldn't even acknowledge their presence. Avon was a very relationship-driven, social organization, so Andrea's occasional frostiness was highly noticeable. She received some early feedback from key leaders about this off-putting behavior, and the cultural emphasis on affiliation helped her develop a more consistently friendly demeanor. She became more comfortable with the Avon standard kiss-on-the-cheek greeting and began opening up to colleagues about personal matters, such as being a mother. Still, she drew the line at discussing her first marriage or her divorce.

Though her aloofness caused some friction, it also conferred a special status upon her that contributed to the development of her aura. During a global marketing meeting in Cancún, some presentations took place outside, where it was very hot and humid. People were sweating and taking off their jackets. Andrea kept her crisp red linen blazer on. Her hair was perfect and she was not sweating. Someone remarked that she must have "air conditioning in her head." It was as if she was not affected by the irritations that beset mere mortals.

Despite this invulnerable aspect, Andrea was vulnerable in other ways early on. As the new kid on the team, she was criticized by veteran executives—some of them treated her harshly, perhaps because they felt threatened by her. Outwardly, she exuded confidence, but she often needed reassurance from her people that she was making the right decision, and on occasion she second-guessed herself.

As Andrea rotated through various marketing positions, she focused on new product development—products that were not only new to the market but also new to the Avon product mix. She created a niche, developing high-tech quality products at a value price. One example was the relaunch and global branding of Anew skin cream, which was the first product in the category to incorporate the cutting-edge alpha hydroxy compound for wrinkles. This successful project was just one illustration of how Andrea could deliver results quickly, earning her a reputation for being effective and innovative.

Jim Preston quickly came to value Andrea's vision, saying, "We looked at the market through one set of glasses. She had a fresh take on what Avon could be."[3] Great leaders often possess a collaborative mindset that creates synergies, and Andrea had this quality from the beginning. For instance, she approached Mattel and CEO Jill Barad in 1994 and suggested a collaborative venture: an Avon Barbie Doll. It became the biggest-selling product launch in Avon's history, with more than 40 million dolls sold. It also led to an instructive friendship—Jill made mistakes and Andrea learned to avoid them from her example It's likely that Jill's great marketing abilities and unique perspective resonated with Andrea. Both women were marketing wunderkinds who revived outdated brands. Both embraced their femininity through their love of fashion and style, unlike some older leaders who adopted more gender-neutral personas.

Andrea was adept at wielding an axe as well as a magic wand. She had no compunction about eliminating older fragrances that were Avon mainstays and replacing them with more contemporary ones such as Far Away, Millennia, and Natori. Andrea had a vision and no fear: "I wanted to revolutionize our image by introducing a new fragrance product, but I could not see why production had to be so expensive. Other companies had a lower cost of goods on a fragrance they were going to sell for $22.00. When I asked why, I learned that we were only using a short production run and every market was using a different bottle."[4]

Despite her relative youth and her status as an outsider working for a company with a deeply entrenched culture and time-honored strategies, Andrea had the courage of her convictions. She was in constant marketing motion. Like Steve Jobs, she got her hands dirty with the details. From creating swiveling lipstick cases to overseeing complete package redesigns for many of the products, Andrea applied her exquisite taste not only to a product's appearance but also to its functionality. In addition, she fired Avon's ad agency and worked to update and globalize Avon's image, launching a new ad slogan, "just another Avon lady."

Further, she personally approved the new shades of lipstick. This may seem like a small thing, but it was indicative of how deep Andrea's commitment was. Employees were incredulous—"Can you believe that Andrea is deciding on shades of lipstick?" Yet this incredulity gave way to admiration as Avon prospered. Gradually, this commitment helped bring people over to her side—it suggested that she indeed was putting the company first despite her glamour and attention-getting personality.

In 1995, earnings climbed 30 percent and sales rose 5 percent. While Andrea wasn't given sole credit for this jump, CEO Preston did say about her, "Here is a person who has the ability to look at the market, envision a plan and execute what she has foreseen."[5]

MARKETING, WOMEN, AND A GLOBAL BRAND

In her embrace of women's causes and integration of them into Avon's marketing efforts, Andrea proved herself to be more than a one-trick pony. Her vision was broader and her skills more multifaceted than the typical marketing executive. For instance, she spearheaded Avon's sponsorship of the 1996 Olympics with two leading women athletes of that era, Jackie Joyner-Kersee and Becky Dyroen-Lancer. Combining product marketing with a focus on women's empowerment and accomplishments, Andrea launched the Olympic Women exhibition, showcasing female athleticism. Andrea described the effort: "We understand women and women's causes and we went out in [a] grassroots effort to teach women and communicate that winning in sports is part of developing self-esteem."[6]

With equal boldness, Andrea launched a new ad campaign—"Dare to Change Your Mind about Avon"—that tackled the touchy issue of Avon being your grandmother's company. The campaign confronted the company's outdated image, making the case successfully that it had changed with the times.

Andrea was nothing if not a contemporary leader. She correctly perceived which issues were important to people in the present, rather than worrying about traditions or past successes. In her embrace of women's issues and her unwillingness to genuflect before sacred cows (i.e., Avon's culture and historical business model), she demonstrated that she was the right leader for Avon at the right time.

Her efforts earned her kudos. *Brandweek* named her Marketer of the Year in 1996 and *Advertising Age* included her in their 1997 list of the top 25 Women to Watch.

But it was her global initiatives that reaped the most praise and that ultimately revealed one of her fatal flaws. Andrea was adamant that Avon develop global brands, based on her strong belief that women everywhere share similar notions of beauty and will buy the same products—that customization based on country and culture was unnecessary. This would allow the company to control quality and create economies of scale, among other benefits.

Yet this global brand approach ignored the need to tailor certain products to a country's particular tastes. The rationale for local sourcing and manufacturing was that management in a given geography could meet the special needs of their customers in that country, retain their margins, and be more nimble in fending off competitors. But Andrea believed that the arguments for a localized approach were too costly and that skimping on product quality could hurt sales and dilute the Avon brand. Andrea believed strongly in the value of quality and consistency, and these requirements had been neglected in a number of countries.

Despite her clear personal preference, Andrea was faced with a classic business paradox—you could muster valid arguments for both the local and global approaches. In *The Unfinished Leader: Balancing Contradictory Answers to Unsolvable Problems,* consultants David Dotlich, Peter Cairo, and Cade Cowan argue that leaders who manage paradox best acknowledge the validity of both sides and develop the agility to make decisions favoring each side as situations warrant.[7]

Andrea, however, was a global brand fundamentalist. In her early years with Avon, this zealous attitude served both her and the company well. By leveraging the organization's capabilities, the company could resource and develop the new generation of high-tech beauty products better than any local country organization could do on its own. As a result, this new global branding strategy was positively received in less well-off countries or in areas where the local organizations were cashstrapped. It allowed Andrea to build a solid power base among Avon groups throughout the world.

In so doing, she seems to have relied on instinct far more than data. In fairness, at the time, Avon's marketing approach was not particularly sophisticated, so there were few analytics to draw upon. She essentially decided that Avon knew best, that rather than responding to what the customers needed or were asking for, they would build it, and the world would beat a path to their door. And in these early years, she was right. Later on though, the pendulum may have swung too far when she became overly reliant on analytics and under-reliant on her intuition.

FROM MARKETING STAR TO CEO CANDIDATE

As Andrea's marketing initiatives succeeded, the skepticism about her receded. Most employees now embraced her as a team player, not a prima donna interested primarily is self-glorification. When she was asked to present to the senior team, she insisted that her team go with her. One former senior leader said that Andrea and her team traveled in a pack. Andrea, of course, took the lead. But her actions helped stamp her as an inclusive leader, which distinguished her from other internal CEO candidates, as did her boldness and ability to catalyze change.

Preston began to see Andrea as a possible successor. He was passionate about Avon and recognized that it was time for a woman to lead it—a woman who was astute about other women and their buying habits. He began to mentor Andrea, giving her board exposure, naming her global marketing head and providing her with overseas activities to bolster her weakness in this area (her entire career up to this point had been in the United States). One such assignment proved to Preston and others in the organization that Andrea could handle these complex international markets with ease.

She was sent to Mexico to oversee a launch of a new product line. A senior Latin American leader (who was not an Andrea supporter) predicted that her trip would be a complete failure. He suggested that Mexican representatives would resent her New York glam appearance and wouldn't connect with her. Yet when Andrea met with these representatives, she charmed them and built a number of good relationships in a very short period of time. The Latin American leader reversed his earlier opinion, sending a glowing report about Andrea's performance to Preston.

While Andrea must have been aware that she was in the running to succeed Preston, she did not engage in overt self-promotion. Instead, she let her achievements and personality do the talking. Sitting on the board of Donna Karan, not to mention her high-profile marriage, generated significant media buzz. It may be that none of these efforts were designed to help her secure the CEO job, but they certainly positioned her as a rising star.

BOARDROOM MANEUVERING

In the 1990s, the CEO succession process was not as structured and rigorous as it is today. Avon had no succession plans, and they didn't formally groom talent to provide a pool of viable candidates. The board's focus was more on finding a quick replacement for Preston if he got hit by the proverbial bus. Preston himself was mentoring Andrea and assuring her that he had bigger things in mind for her, but there were no specific plans. In addition, Andrea, despite hitting the ground running and achieving impossible-to-ignore achievements, still had the Old Guard to deal with—senior executives who had put in their time and felt they were more deserving of the CEO job than she was.

When Preston announced that he wanted to retire, the board asked him to postpone leaving until they could launch a search to find the next CEO. The board stated their criteria and emphasized the importance of finding someone who had "been there, done that." Though Andrea was a candidate, she had never been a CEO before, which was a strike against her. At the same time, the board made it clear that they wanted someone who could build a global brand, was a cultural fit, and could inspire Avon's vast network of representatives. Andrea's bold strategy and vision to contemporize the brand almost seemed to have shaped the board's criteria, lending credibility to her candidacy despite her lack of CEO experience.

The board drew up a list of internal and external candidates, the former including Andrea, Susan Kropf, and Joe Ferreira, now the head of Avon's international group. Because Preston had promoted women into executive roles and placed Andrea on the fast track, people assumed that the next CEO would be a woman. Though Christina Gold had been another front-runner for the job before the board began its formal process, she had turned down a job managing operations in other countries to take on a staff position as head of global direct selling, a role that she perceived as critical for the organization's future. Inadvertently, Christina had removed herself from consideration for the top spot because of this move—staff positions were suddenly becoming dead ends for executives, especially women executives, because at that time line roles were viewed as the most critical. Christina left the company and went on to have an even more successful career at other companies, most notably spearheading the turnaround of Western Union.

Though board member Brenda Barnes publicly stated that the board would have liked to have found a woman to take on the CEO position, the best-qualified candidate turned out to be a man. Charlie Perrin, an Avon board member since 1996, had been CEO of Duracell and had taken that company's market cap from $1.8 billion to $9.4 billion over a four-year period. The board also found that he had strong interpersonal skills and related well to women in management positions.

Though he met the specs identified by the board for Avon CEO, his appointment was controversial. At the time, the number of women heading major companies in the United States was small, and pressure was mounting throughout the country for boards to name women CEOs when appropriate. Because of Avon's status as "a company for women," appointing a female CEO seemed like a no-brainer. When this didn't come to pass, many women were upset, including Andrea.

It turned into a public relations nightmare for the company, as media pundits raised the possibility of discrimination. Because of her high marketability, Andrea could have easily left Avon in her disappointment and taken another position. In fact, she had two CEO offers from other companies after Charlie Perrin was selected.

Why Andrea turned down these offers and decided to remain at Avon is an object lesson in the value of patience. I'm not suggesting that all senior people who are passed over for top positions should stay where they are and wait their turn. In some instances, being passed over is a sign that your time with a given company is up—that you'll never move any higher no matter what you do or how circumstances change. But the key is to analyze the situation carefully rather than acting out of anger or disappointment.

Astutely, Andrea talked to Avon Board member and Time CEO Ann Moore about what she should do. She needed a clear-headed, objective perspective, and Ann provided it. Andrea frequently recounted Ann's advice to: "Follow your compass, not your clock. Make the decision from your heart, not your head." Andrea recalled this advice, and her subsequent decision to stay: "I had fallen in love with what Avon does. I realized I would far prefer to be number two in a company with this potential impact on society than to be number one in another company without that kind of impact. If you don't love what you do, it is too great a sacrifice. This is not a women's issue, it is true for men and women alike."[8]

As ambitious as Andrea was, her ultimate goal was not the CEO title. Instead, she yearned to do something for the greater good. She wanted to make her mark, to implement her vision in a way that would have an impact. While her ticking career clock and her appreciation of being offered a CEO spot might have tempted her to leave, her career direction and heart told her to stay. Avon represented an unprecedented opportunity to put her vision for a company into practice. It provided her with a chance to help women in multiple ways around the world, from giving them better ways to make a living to creating a foundation dedicated to women's causes such as breast cancer and spousal abuse.

So Andrea stayed, with the promise that she would be Charlie's number two executive and also receive a seat on the board. Andrea's decision to stay turned out to be a wise one. For one thing, Andrea recognized that she needed to develop herself in a number of ways to be better prepared for a CEO position. For instance, she wanted to serve on an external board, and shortly after Charlie was named CEO, a spot on GE's board opened up that they wanted to fill with a rising female leader. It was the perfect board for Andrea, in that she had a chance to learn from and work with Jack Welch and see how one of the world's best-run companies operated.

She also gained valuable global experience during this period, especially in operations, as well as the opportunity to take on spotlight roles—she traveled around the world and spoke to high-level groups just as a CEO might. Looking back, Andrea recognized how worthwhile these experiences were because her past experience had been limited to US-based marketing. The board insisted that she go on the road and get some of the operations and international experience that was needed.

MAKING THE BEST OF A BAD SITUATION

While the board believed that the pairing of Andrea and Charlie would be synergistic and sustainable, it was at best tolerable and temporary. At first, their disparate strengths seemed to be working in Avon's favor. Charlie focused on reducing costs through process reengineering and on refining the incentive program for sales representatives. Andrea concentrated on testing a retail selling strategy and image-enhancement programs with the launch of the Avon Centre, a 20,000-square-foot retail operation and spa located in New York's Trump Tower at a cost of $5 million. She also helped implement a plan to set up retail kiosks in malls and lease them to Avon representatives.

Andrea's ventures were expensive and created some grumbling among senior staff. Some questioned her commitment to the direct-selling channel. Still, at this point in her career at Avon, she had been so extraordinarily successful that she could weather the grumbling.

Charlie was not so lucky. Like many external senior hires, he underestimated the direct-selling learning curve and struggled to adjust to running a company so dependent on direct sales. One former senior leader said that at times Charlie was anxious about his position in the company relative to Andrea's. His anxiety was understandable, as the board and others in the company may well have favored her over him. As one senior leader told me, "Charlie always thought she had a direct line to the board members and used this as a way to undermine him." In fact, she did nothing of the kind, but she also didn't dispel his concern. I'm not sure if Andrea intimidated him, but he no doubt noticed that she was garnering much more attention than him, both inside and outside the company. It didn't help that morale was low, as were earnings and the share price. Charlie resigned in less than two years, and the board acted quickly to appoint Andrea CEO. Though some thought Susan Kropf deserved the job, most felt that Andrea was in the best position to lead the company out of its doldrums.

Before we leave this period, it's worth noting that though Andrea could have taken the opportunity to turn people against Charlie and pressure the board to get rid of him and appoint her CEO earlier, she never did. Perhaps a man would have seen the situation in Darwinian terms and plotted to get rid of Charlie, but Andrea waited patiently for things to work themselves out. Again, she probably heard her father's voice in her head, counseling patience. She may have recognized that Charlie's tenure as CEO was doomed, and she was willing to let events take their course. In this way, no one could accuse her of being manipulative or cutthroat; the last thing she wanted to do was alienate board members and others who had brought Charlie into the company.

Conversely, Charlie and Andrea's problematic relationship prevented Andrea from developing expertise in operations. Initially, the plan was for Charlie to coach Andrea in this area, helping her become a more well-rounded leader. Unfortunately, this never happened to the extent that it should have. At the time of her appointment as CEO, this lack of operations knowledge didn't seem a major problem for Avon or for Andrea.

LEADERSHIP LESSONS LEARNED

1. *Find the match between leaders' talents and an organization's opportunities.* Andrea could have found better positions at bigger companies than Avon when she left Neiman Marcus. But consciously or not, she realized that Avon represented an ideal situation for her. The opportunity was more than the position. She could have made more money and acquired a more prestigious title, office, and other perks elsewhere. But Avon needed someone exactly like Andrea—someone with branding skills, style, and a vision. Not every job would have allowed her to put all these elements into practice. Finding this match is partly instinctive, but it also requires astute assessment of what an organization needs and what it will allow you to do. At the most basic level, Andrea recognized that an organization that marketed to women would eventually name a woman as CEO—probably sooner than later. More subtly, she also grasped that there would be an opportunity to work with senior staff from the start to communicate her vision and demonstrate her talents.

2. *Encourage strategic boldness.* Andrea wasn't shy about stating her views, and Avon not only accepted her aggressive initiatives but rewarded her for them. Her willingness to

recommend dramatic changes in Avon's image and product mix risked seeming presumptuous, especially to conservative veterans of the company who still considered
Andrea an outsider. But Andrea wasn't obnoxious in her
presentation, and she didn't overstep her mandate. Instead,
she chose the right moments to be bold—meetings, presentations, and key one-on-ones. In this way, she ensured
everyone knew that she was innovative, smart, and aggressive—traits that stuck in people's minds even if they didn't
always agree with her ideas.

3. *Plug the gaps in knowledge and skills.* As noted earlier, Andrea
   identified the gaps in her own knowledge with the help of
   Preston and other senior leaders. She knew she had to gain
   global experience, get outside her marketing function, and
   learn to lead a wide range of people on an international
   stage. The time between Preston's and Charlie Perrin's retirements offered Andrea a window to fill at least some of
   her gaps. Andrea was in danger of falling into a trap that
   catches many young and rising stars, especially women: as-
   cending through a function but never developing significant
   skills and knowledge outside of that function. Instead, they
   get typecast as a marketing person or a financial expert or
   an IT guy. Most organizations, however, expect individuals
   who are candidates for top jobs to have taken on line roles
   with some profit and loss (P&L) responsibility. Many companies, too, want their people not only to gain management
   responsibility over other countries but to have a two- to
   three-year assignment working in a country other than their
   own. While Andrea plugged some of her gaps, she didn't
   plug all of them, and that became a problem later on in her
   career. There are various ways to fill these gaps. Andrea, for

instance, never received an MBA; instead, she used board members and mentors to foster the learning she needed. Training programs, stretch assignments, and other methods are all fine for gap-filling. Organizations should understand, though, that when leaders display a special talent such as Andrea did for marketing, their bosses may resist granting them the time and opportunity they require to educate themselves in other disciplines. Preston, for instance, rotated Andrea through various marketing assignments since that was her sweet spot, where she would deliver the most immediate value to the company. Organizations may need to fill the gaps in counterintuitive ways—giving leaders the chance to work in areas where they're lacking rather than in areas where they possess natural abilities.

4. *Follow your compass, not your clock.* This advice, which Andrea received from Avon Board member Ann Moore, is something every leader at a career turning point should consider and that every organization should etch above the entrance to the human resources department. Women in their thirties may hear the ticking of their biological clocks; budding leaders at the same age hear the ticking of their career clocks. They are so eager to advance that they sometimes jump at the wrong jobs or react with anger rather than thoughtfulness when they're passed over. Andrea sought advice and reflected deeply as she considered leaving Avon when she was passed over for the CEO position. She talked about what she really wanted from a job and a career, what impact she wanted to have, what legacy she wanted to leave. Her compass told her to stay, even as her clock may have told her she was falling behind. Seeking sage advice and making time for honest and deep reflection is the way

to find this compass and not be a slave to a ticking career clock. The advice that Andrea always gave to young leaders was, "The infectiousness of your leadership must be apparent to the people, or you can't charge forward. If you don't love it, you can't fake it."[9]

THREE

A GREAT FIRST IMPRESSION

1999–2000

SOME NEWLY MINTED CEOS STEP INTO THE ROLE WITH CAUTION AND MODERATION; THEY don't want to make a huge mistake right off the bat. In the spotlight for perhaps the first time, they are hesitant to take risks until they've figured out the lay of the land.

Andrea had more reason than most to take it slowly. At the time of her appointment, only three other Fortune 500 companies had female CEOs. As strange as it may seem now, in 1999 the jury was still out as to whether a woman could be the successful head of a major corporation. Jill Barad was struggling at Mattel, as was Carly Fiorina at Hewlett Packard, while Marion Sandler at Golden West Financial (her family's business) successfully continued in her frugal and modest way. As the first female head of the "company for women," Andrea was under tremendous scrutiny. But she was not a slow and careful leader. She was bold and willing to take reasonable risks, and from the moment she assumed the top job at Avon, she embraced the moment. She refused to be cowed by the watching world or her own lack of experience as CEO. She must have recognized that she was the perfect person for the position. In fact, when Stanley Gault, the lead director of Avon's board, called at 10:00 p.m. and told her that she had been named CEO, Andrea woke her young daughter, Lauren, to tell her the news. Lauren responded sleepily, "Mommy, go back to sleep. You must be dreaming."[1]

It was indeed a dream job, and Andrea turned that dream into a great reality for herself and the company.

A SERIES OF CHALLENGES

When Andrea became CEO, many employees were excited by what felt like a historical moment, and just about everyone was rooting for her to succeed. The announcement set off a media storm that culminated in Dan Rather of *CBS News* showing up at Avon headquarters to interview Andrea. The buzz was loud, and the expectations were high.

Tempering all this excitement, however, were Avon's business struggles. At the time of Andrea's appointment, the share price had hit a three-year low of $25 (down from a high of $55), and takeover rumors swirled for the second time in Avon's history. Though the stock rose a bit in response to her being named CEO, Wall Street was cautious.

Her first challenge, then, was a November 1999 meeting with analysts in which she reaffirmed the transformation strategy that she had worked on with Charlie Perrin before he departed. Remarkably, she was entirely composed, seeming to relish the chance to make her case for Avon and reveal her plans. Her performance was mesmerizing, and the analysts emerged far more supportive than combative. When Andrea left the room, the beginnings of a halo were starting to glow above her head.

Still, the challenges kept coming, and they were formidable:

- *Determining how to leverage economies of scale without alienating the local General Managers.* The organization was confused about the globalization strategy that had been laid out under Charlie Perrin. To the various country general managers around the world, "globalization" translated into being told what to do by corporate. There was skepticism from the local markets as well as confusion about roles and accountabilities. It was already clear that Avon's future growth would be driven by the international markets. In the past, the Avon markets had operated very autonomously and wielded enormous power. Andrea needed the support and alignment of the leaders in these markets. They needed to understand what globalization really meant and wanted to see the business case for it.

- *Establishing how to contemporize the direct-selling channel.* This was a major challenge, especially in mature markets like the United States. The Internet was rapidly become an effective selling tool, and more Avon customers were clicking their mouses than answering their doorbells. So how could Avon leverage the Internet without offending the representatives who sold door-to-door? The question was further complicated by Andrea's perception of retail as a key growth driver for the United States. On top of all that, direct selling remained a highly effective sales approach in many foreign markets.

  But other direct-selling companies outside of the United States were offering more competitive representative earnings opportunities. Avon had already piloted some alternative earnings models, and Andrea knew that finding the right model would be crucial.

- *Updating Avon's image and building brands.* The company desperately needed new advertising, products, packaging, and brochures, but this would cost a great deal of money they didn't have at the time. In order to free up resources, she would need to accelerate the Business Process Redesign (BPR) program begun in 1997 as a way to streamline processes as well as take out cost to reinvest.

- *Assessing overseas markets.* Everyone agreed that future growth would be tied to countries such as China, Russia, and India. Yet Avon needed to find the right strategy for these markets—not an easy task.

- *Fixing broken processes.* As late as 1999, Avon representatives had to rely on paper-and-pencil forms (often 40 pages of them) for ordering products. Not only was this process time-consuming and cumbersome, but it often resulted in incomplete or incorrect orders. This and other processes needed to be fixed, but doing so would be costly, and the transitions would require time and education.

- *Evolving the culture while still retaining an entrepreneurial spirit.* The latter defined and drove Avon's people, but major changes were needed, and some of those changes risked destroying morale and driving people out of the company. Charlie Perrin had started down this path, with mostly negative results. Andrea knew these changes had to be made, but how far could she go, and how fast? Was such an evolution even possible with the people she had in place? Avon had a reputation as a fun and friendly place to work where individual initiative was prized, yet it was also known for lacking structure, discipline, and focus. So while Andrea was committed to evolving the culture, she worried about the consequences and questioned whether she even had the right talent pool and processes to facilitate it.

Most new CEOs face major obstacles and ambitious goals, but this list might give even the most seasoned leaders pause. Andrea recognized that she could never deal with all the issues on her plate without the support of key people throughout the organization. Consciously or not, she decided to lead in the most natural way possible from the very beginning. Rather than adopting a particular leadership persona, Andrea relied on her authenticity, which ultimately helped her craft a highly effective public image.

MEETING THE CHALLENGES NATURALLY

Some leaders seem to know, from the moment they are crowned, who they want to be. Their authenticity becomes an asset as they project a consistent, compelling image year after year. Andrea embodied this principle from the moment she took over. She made a conscious choice to remain authentic in her leadership style, avoiding some of the mistakes that other female CEOs had made.

She didn't want to be a celebrity CEO like Carly Fiorina, and she eschewed media interviews that focused on nonbusiness topics like fashion or the social scene as well as those who wanted to profile her as a feminist pioneer. Andrea was all about the business, and she made that clear early on. Unlike Jill Barad, who made headlines for showing up for a business meeting in a Barbie doll-like hot pink jumpsuit, Andrea stuck to a strictly professional style—albeit an expensive, designer one. Some thought that Andrea might trade in her pearls and high-priced outfits for something that the typical Avon lady could more easily relate to, but she continued to dress to the nines. This was part of her personality, what people had come to expect, and to go another way would have been inauthentic.

Though Andrea had no interest in the external trappings of a celebrity CEO, she quickly became a celebrity among Avon's employees. She was modeling the woman that Avon representatives could aspire to be—glamorous, smart, and successful. When Andrea attended her first Avon representative convention, the reps greeted her with tremendous enthusiasm, asking her to pose with them for photos and sign autographs.

Andrea was also astute about creating a broadly inclusive inner circle. Typically, new CEOs seek out a few key people who they can depend upon for advice or to carry out key tasks. Andrea was quick to create this circle, identifying colleagues who could supply the knowledge or skills that she lacked—she was more aware than many leaders of her own weaknesses, and she was willing to delegate others to handle these areas. But unlike most CEOs, membership in Andrea's circle was a matter of perception—scores of people assumed they were in it. And in a way, they were right. Andrea made her people feel special. It was a deceptively brilliant use of a normally exclusionary tool.

Typically, leaders build up their people by giving them challenging assignments and rewarding them for successful execution, using everything from compliments to bonuses. Certainly Andrea did some of this, but her way of creating committed followership was more subtle—and perhaps more effective—than traditional methods. She treated her direct reports, not just as employees, but as confidantes. There was nothing forced or artificial about this—it was her natural method of relating to people she liked and valued. Once, when she was being interviewed for a Vogue spread, they brought her an entire rack of clothes to try on. She came into my office shortly thereafter and started talking about how all the clothes were too small for her and how thin models must be. It wasn't typical CEO behavior—it was more like a conversation sisters might have. On more than one occasion, Andrea would go into my boss's office, grab a snack, sit down and vent, dish, or express her uncertainty about a decision. Her willingness to be vulnerable was endearing, balancing the strength and confidence she projected in so many situations. Andrea wasn't trying to be everyone's friend—her paradoxically aloof nature prevented that—but her ability to occasionally relax, confide in, and complain to members of her team drew people to her side and kept them loyal.

Just as her vulnerability created loyalty, so too did her fierce intelligence. People returned from meetings with Andrea energized and glowing with purpose. Part of it was that Andrea was adept at helping people lift their thinking to the next level; she encouraged her colleagues to tease out thoughts and examine them from fresh angles. She was also often several steps ahead of everyone else in the room but never let on. Of course, it didn't hurt that she was already moving in elite social circles. She often had great stories to tell about the people she had met. For a while, I helped her draft speeches on leading a global organization to various groups, primarily because it gave me more one-on-one time with her; it was both fun and educational. The men in the organization were particularly in Andrea's thrall; they worked hard to get her attention and basked in her praise. We used to say that the guys "wanted to make mommy proud," even though Andrea was not a classic maternal type. Everyone wanted to please her, yet there was little in-fighting during the first five or six years she was CEO—the Avon culture combined with Andrea's leadership style prevented this type of gamesmanship.

Despite the varying perceptions of her inner circle, Andrea relied most heavily on Avon's top two executives: Joe Ferreira and Susan Kropf. They functioned as co-COOs, with Joe responsible for international and Susan for operations. This setup had some problematic aspects—Joe was still unhappy that he had been passed over for the CEO position. But it was a necessary troika, as Andrea was well aware that she needed help securing the support of the global markets and operations—her two Achilles heels—to succeed. And for the first year, it worked well, allowing Andrea to shine as the external face of the organization while two highly competent individuals managed the nitty-gritty details behind the scenes.

A TRICKY STRATEGY

During her first year as CEO, Andrea faced a number of business challenges, but the overarching issue was change. It was clear that Avon had to emerge from its financial funk and set up a path for growth. Andrea's predecessor, Charlie Perrin, along with McKinsey and Company strategy consultants had mapped out the necessary moves to achieve these objectives. The thrust of their recommendations was to focus on several key strategies for growth, walking the tightrope between leveraging economies of scale while retaining Avon's core entrepreneurial spirit and market nimbleness. They also recommended cleaning up some of the broken processes and freeing up funds for reinvestment.

Though Andrea recognized the value of a more directive approach, she was also keenly aware of the dangers, that is, alienating Avon's overseas markets. At this point, the US market accounted for 60 percent of Avon's sales, but all future growth was projected overseas, with those markets set to generate the majority of sales in the near future. Andrea grasped that the change must be gradual and accommodate overseas markets as well as those in the United States. So she crystallized the existing strategy, focusing on creating more integrated businesses and leveraging economies of scale while at the same time accommodating local markets (customizing products and policies to fit the different conditions in countries like China and Russia).

Andrea's new strategy was a reflection of her own personality as an innovative marketer and her belief that a stronger, more contemporary worldwide brand would lead to future growth. She is often credited with wanting to accomplish this through what became known as "masstige"—products that are technology driven and high quality but affordable. The research and design (R&D) arm of the organization would play a key role in creating more quality, high-tech brands that could sell at lower prices.

At the time, some observers—as well as a few veterans within Avon—thought that this strategy was too upscale for the traditional Avon customer—the old-fashioned, 50-plus woman. But Andrea believed Avon could become a brand for a more diverse group, including trendy, young, and more affluent women. More than that, she believed fervently that women deserved high-quality, technologically sophisticated products at affordable prices.

Andrea was passionate about her woman-centric vision for the company, saying, "We are not in the business of selling lipsticks through a direct-sales channel. We are in the business of changing women's lives." "I see us having a very unique proposition," she maintained, "in that Avon has got a social purpose as well as a commercial purpose to changing women's lives."[2]

CEOs—especially strong, charismatic ones—often possess deeply held beliefs that, consciously or not, shape their business decisions. Andrea was a classy lady with an upscale mentality. She rarely acknowledged that Avon's core representatives and customers tended to be from the lower end of the socioeconomic spectrum. At one of the US representative conventions shortly after Andrea became CEO, Richard Simmons was one of the featured celebrities, dancing to the oldies on stage with mostly overweight representatives. In awkward deference to Andrea's vision for a "hipper" representative, some of the staff were trying to find a better mix of younger, thinner representatives for him to dance with. It was almost as if Andrea refused to get bogged down by past perceptions of Avon, even if they still represented the current reality, so determined was she to keep her vision front and center.

Image was important to Andrea, so it wasn't surprising that one of her first major strategic initiatives was corporate image enhancement. In that first year on the job, Andrea announced a 50-percent spending increase for a worldwide ad campaign titled "Let's Talk." Andrea was well aware of the advertising done by local Avon groups in China, Russia, Brazil, Poland, and the Philippines—the company's overseas growth areas—and thought much of it was "schlocky." But she was diplomatic in announcing the new campaign, especially with country heads—she framed it in forward-looking terms, talking about the need for a consistent, high-quality message.

The "Let's Talk" campaign was the first global advertising campaign launched in 20 countries. The ads showcased the Avon brand, but also Avon's unique relationship with women. It was translated into multiple languages, and the models featured in each spot came from the countries in which they ran. Andrea had a clear plan for the worldwide image, but despite her zealous belief in it, she made a slow, sometimes painstaking effort to secure buy-in and obtain input from global staff to ensure all ideas were heard. In the end, the campaign was a success that generated sales growth, as well as a rise in the number of new and active representatives. Part of Avon's image problem involved "knickknacks"—nonbeauty, home products that Avon reps sold in both the US and foreign markets. Andrea wanted to prune the product line so that the company could focus more on beauty and thus get its image and margins in line with her vision for Avon. Yet there were problems with her plan. Most of these nonbeauty items generated sales and excitement among customers—the fiber-optic Christmas trees, for instance, were huge sellers during the holidays. The margins for these items were low, however, making it difficult to estimate what items were going to be the hits or misses of the season. These items also created an identity crisis for Avon—are we a beauty company or a direct-selling company? For a direct-selling company, the channel was the focus. For example, Avon's operation in Brazil was the biggest seller of shoes in that country. At one point in Argentina the reps sold automobile tires! To insist they sell only beauty products would alienate the reps in those countries and potentially damage revenue. And in the United States, reps often did good business by selling at flea markets—the opposite of the upscale image Andrea was pursuing.

Andrea also found herself in a bind that faces many new leaders of old companies: confronting traditions that no longer work in the face of emerging realities. Even early in her tenure, Andrea grappled with whether Avon was a beauty company or a direct selling one. Such a critical question, yet it had no easy answer. The traditional direct-selling channel was what made Avon the company it was. Beauty was a growth industry for the future, especially in markets outside of the United States. Would an upscale woman in New York or Chicago buy from Avon when it sold many products in a blue-collar, door-to-door approach? Perhaps even more significant, where would upscale customers in New York or Chicago buy these products in the future? Would the company be able to compete with the top beauty companies if it forsook its enormously powerful, company-defining sales technique?

Not all of Andrea's initiatives were so problematic. Many of her image-based improvements were essential and productive, such as redesigning brochures so they reflected quality, especially outside the United States. Her decision to drive growth through new categories such as wellness, hair care, and jewelry was well received. She launched a business-to-business Internet strategy that allowed representatives to be more productive and responsive to customers; Avon estimated that it cost them one dollar to process a paper order and only 20 cents for an online order.

Boldness is probably the best word to characterize Andrea's initiatives during that first year. Given all the programs she implemented, you would think that she was a veteran leader of a company in a strong market position, not the first-time CEO of a company beset by a low stock price and great uncertainty. Andrea, though, never hesitated to pull the trigger on innovative projects. She made a significant investment in developing affordable but technologically advanced products by increasing the R&D budget by 46 percent. Recall that she had almost simultaneously increased ad expenditures by 50 percent; she was not shy about taking risks when it made strategic sense to do so.

In a matter of months, Andrea also started a program designed to deliver better support services to Avon reps as well as provide them with increased compensation for recruiting and training other reps. Her initial strategy also called for pushing the company to develop new customer segments such as a teen business and making a plunge into retail—but this push didn't take place until much later.

On top of all this, Andrea began implementing her philanthropic vision for Avon. Her grandmother had died from breast cancer, and she saw an opportunity for the Avon Foundation to generate increased funding for research to combat this disease through walks and other events. The Avon Foundation had been created in 1955 with a focus on education and job training. The shift to breast cancer actually began in the United Kingdom in 1992. Andrea wanted to accelerate the funding as well as replicate the breast cancer focus in other countries. She set a lofty objective: to eradicate breast cancer forever. Since 1999, $175 million had been funded for breast cancer research, and through 2012, more than $910 million has been raised by the Avon Foundation in more than 50 countries. Former Avon Foundation staff said that she embarked on this crusade because it was the right thing to do and that she was not looking for any type of financial or business return. Andrea personally called doctors at breast cancer facilities that Avon supported when female staff were diagnosed with the disease.

THE TOP 100: MOBILIZING THE ORGANIZATION

Some leaders talk a great game but struggle when it comes to execution. What made Andrea so successful that first year was that she had the vision but was also savvy enough to surround herself with the talent to execute it. Like many CEOs, she preferred creating the strategy and obtaining buy-in to getting her hands dirty implementing the details. Andrea saw that she had to build a critical mass of core leaders who would be committed to executing her vision—without them, she could not be successful. Avon was a relationship-driven, tight-knit corporate community, and unlike more hierarchical, command-and-control companies, leaders at Avon needed consensus to get things done.

To that end, the senior vice president of human resources (along with myself) helped identify the most senior and critical 100 leaders at Avon who were dubbed "agents of change." The goal was to align and mobilize this group of key influencers to drive the company's agenda. Early on in Andrea's tenure, we held a series of off-sites for this group. They included education sessions on globalization with top gurus with an eye toward giving the organization a common language to discuss what globalization was and wasn't and what it meant for Avon. They also included, 360-degree feedback on leadership behaviors deemed critical to the transformation's success. And they incorporated Wall Street analysts offering their views on Avon's strengths and weaknesses as well as intense back-and-forth discussions with Andrea, Susan, and Joe.

In these early years, Andrea was never at a loss for new ideas. At times it was all we could do to keep up with her churning mind. To ensure that she was able to monitor all the ideas percolating at higher levels throughout the organization, Andrea launched a CEO advisory council composed of ten high-potential leaders from offices around the world who met quarterly and offered her insights about the organization.

Besides getting advice and buy-in from Avon's top leaders, Andrea knew she had to create a more performance-based culture. In the late 1990s, this was the prized model—results-focused, disciplined, rigorously analytic, with clear lines of accountability and world-class talent. It was also the type of culture that consultants recommended to their clients and that former CEO Charlie Perrin and Andrea had agreed to build. Yet Andrea had observed Charlie's efforts in that direction and the ensuing rebellion. She knew that some Avon people felt Charlie was suggesting that the existing culture was low-performance, despite significant, positive results just prior to the recent economic downturn in 1999.

But Andrea had served on Jack Welch's board at General Electric, and the experience affected the way she strategized. She knew that she needed to drive the cultural change herself, but did not want to fall into the trap that Charlie had. So she drove the change in two ways: first, through a revised performance management system, and second, through a revised bonus system. At GE, Welch favored tough love and grading performance along a bell curve, so that in any given year you would have 20 percent extremely high performers, 70 percent average or acceptable performers, and about 10 percent unacceptable performers. The latter group would be placed on a performance improvement plan or managed out of the organization. Andrea set up a similar system at Avon. Welch viewed himself as both a change agent and chief HR/talent officer, and Andrea modeled her approach after that. When she announced the new system, it elicited protests from a number of veteran Avon executives as well as the internal human resource community who thought that it was too much, too soon for managers who weren't especially sophisticated about performance objectives. But Andrea stood her ground, and it paid dividends by rewarding outstanding results and punishing subpar ones.

Although Andrea grasped intellectually that she had to model the changes that she was requiring of others, she struggled with the concept behaviorally; her pleaser derailer got in the way of walking the talk. At times, she would agree to make a tough decision related to performance—telling people that they needed to be more enterprise-focused, for instance, or refusing to give them an expected bonus—and then she would "blink." This was actually the word people used within the executive ranks to describe Andrea's refusal to follow through on a performance-related decision. Members of the senior team gave her clear feedback on this and even volunteered to help her craft the more difficult messages and think through worst-case scenarios. Sometimes this helped, but it was an ongoing struggle.

At the time, though, the organization could tolerate her occasional inability to tell people bad news. Andrea was reshaping the culture in other ways that were highly effective, and realigning the performance management process was one of them. She drew a clear line between strategic priorities and rewards and recognitions—or punishments. Andrea might have had trouble doing this sort of thing in one-on-one interactions, but she was able and eager to do it systematically. In the past, Avon, like many other companies, had been lax in this area; most people received average reviews in the middle of the range. The amiability of the culture tolerated mediocre performance, and many managers routinely shied away from tough conversations—just like Andrea.

THE AURA BEGINS TO SHIMMER

If Andrea's halo started to glow during her first meeting with analysts, it really started to sparkle in the ensuing months when she could apparently do no wrong. When Andrea was first named CEO, the board had requested that its chairman, the former CEO of Rubbermaid, Stanley Gault, mentor and guide her through her initial months on the job. But it became clear almost immediately that Andrea required no guidance. She was born to the job, and while she may have needed support in some areas, she was eminently capable of leading Avon on her own.

Typically, new CEOs are under the microscope. Andrea, as both a woman and a first-time CEO of Avon, was being watched more closely than most. Despite this intense scrutiny, no obvious flaw emerged, no significant mistakes were made. Remarkably, most of her decisions during that first year were the right ones, and the numbers bear that out (the following are two-year totals, but the increases were readily apparent in her first year). Annual sales growth was 1.5 percent in 1999 when Andrea became CEO, and it rose to 6 percent in 2001. Avon's share price shot up to a 52-week high of $50 in 2001, an amazing 70 percent two-year increase. The total number of Avon sales reps increased from 3 million to 3.5 million during this period, and in 2001 Andrea was named chairperson of Avon's board.

But the numbers are only one measure of Andrea's early success. Lots of CEOs deliver good numbers but never develop the aura of a superstar. When she launched her turnaround strategy, Andrea became a global presence, both for rescuing a well-known company that had been in trouble and as an inspiration to other women. It seemed you couldn't pick up a magazine during this time without finding a profile of her. Beautiful, smart, poised, and charismatic, Andrea was made for the media. In her interviews, she consistently shared credit with her team, endearing herself to her top people. When she spoke at internal meetings or gave external talks, she was eloquent and persuasive. The energy she created was palpable—she won over the naysayers and doubters, and soon everyone from the board to the representatives was behind her 100 percent.

Having two COOs turned out not to be a workable model with the organization needing a more unified structure. Consequently, co-COO Joe Ferreira left the organization in January 2001. After his departure, Andrea's relationship with Susan Kropf appeared to flourish. She was the ideal COO, complementing Andrea in many ways. Avon employees referred to them as the "ying and yang" of the organization. Andrea was the strategic visionary, while Susan took care of the quotidian details of running the company. Andrea would come up with ten new ideas for growth and Susan would then say, "We have $10 million we can invest: What are your top two?" You could sometimes hear their heated discussions wafting through the corridors, but they always battled it out in private, and their mutual respect never wavered. Susan had started at Avon as a secretary right after college and worked her way up through the organization, taking on a great diversity of roles and even making the time to earn an MBA in finance along the way. One of her former staff gave Susan a present of a rubber dog bone one year, signifying her tenaciousness: she could gnaw on an issue like the proverbial dog with a bone. She knew the company inside and out and worked with great focus to understand the root cause of any problem. She didn't hesitate to call one of the regional heads or country managers and ask a follow-up question when she spotted a buried, but telling, number at the end of a PowerPoint deck. Susan and Andrea developed a rhythm and precision in their roles rarely seen between a leader and her second in command. Too often, this relationship devolves over time due to stress, jealously, or competitiveness. Susan always seemed content to be in Andrea's shadow. They never appeared to compete with each other. Andrea always spoke highly of her in public, and vice versa.

LEADERSHIP LESSONS LEARNED

1. *Seek leaders who can be both architects of change and its driver.* Being a visionary leader is great, but it's not enough. Just as some entrepreneurs are brilliant at coming up with ideas for new companies but terrible at running the companies they create, so too are some leaders great a creating new strategies and bad at executing them. Andrea was instinctively astute about how to create change and then empower people to execute it. She saw her role as driving change through the company. She didn't shy away from the difficult aspects of

implementation. When the compensation and bonus plan were realigned and the performance management process adjusted (so that there was a greater emphasis on measuring and rewarding performance), Andrea stepped up and confronted the questions and criticism these changes provoked. Like Jack Welch, she took ownership of decisions related to talent, especially regarding new roles for country leaders. Like a good politician, she went out on the road and gave stump speeches for the changes she was advocating. In a very real way, her involvement in Avon's changes was wide and deep. This isn't to say that she did everything perfectly—as I noted earlier, she struggled with the cultural changes required. But whether instinctively or by following Jack Welch's example, Andrea saw that she had to take complete ownership of the new programs and policies she was proposing. Doing so communicates, both internally and externally, how serious you are about the changes; it allows you to walk the talk, and it makes you the hero if the changes prove to be successful.

2. *Balance decisiveness with inclusion.* This is a hard lesson for many leaders to learn. Some are relentlessly decisive—they make quick, unilateral choices believing that it demonstrates their strength as a leader. Others strive for participatory decision making, soliciting ideas and information from as diverse a populace as possible. There's nothing wrong with either approach, but when one becomes the exclusive operating mode, it weakens leaders. As we've seen, Andrea created an expansive inner circle, one that caused far more senior leaders than the norm to believe that their ideas were listened to and acted upon. She brought many of the disenchanted representatives back into the fold as well as other employees throughout the company. At the same time, she didn't recoil

from making tough decisions, such as insisting on a stronger performance management system. Being able to integrate both decisiveness and inclusiveness into her management style was crucial for Andrea's early success, as it can be for any leader who is able to recognize both approaches.

3. *Keep the focus on the company rather than the individual.* Admittedly, there's a fine line that must be walked here. CEOs tend to have healthy egos, and many have capitalized on their charisma to help their organizations. But when CEOs make it all about their brilliance, they ultimately do themselves and their organizations a disservice. When things go south, as they invariably do given enough time, then the CEO reaps all the blame (since he or she has made it all about himself or herself). More significantly, this overly self-centered CEO creates resentment in the ranks and fails to position the organizational strategy effectively—everything seems secondary to the CEO's superior insights and skills. Fortunately, Andrea was able to see how other CEOs and senior leaders—especially women—suffered when they focused attention on their beauty and brains. In media interviews, analyst meetings, and elsewhere, she talked about Avon, about "we," about the company's strengths. This elevated the organization, and of course, Andrea rose with it.

4. *Spotlight the vital few rather than the trivial many.* In terms of execution, leaders—especially younger, highly ambitious leaders—often float so many initiatives that it's difficult for people to know where to concentrate. They launch one terrific strategy after the next, generating excitement and commitment initially but losing momentum when people struggle to figure out where they should focus their energy. During her first year as CEO, Andrea created a disciplined process with

her senior team that set clear goals and metrics so that her key people knew what they were accountable for and how their work fit into larger organizational strategy. She also created a one-page poster that summarized her first-year CEO agenda, giving people a snapshot of top priorities. In this way, Andrea was able to concentrate a tremendous amount of effort on a relatively small number of objectives, increasing the odds that they would be achieved.

5. *Esteem authenticity.* Organizations run by leaders who are genuinely themselves often excel, a reflection of the aura that surrounds those leaders. Andrea never tried to be anyone other than who she really was. Unlike other neophyte CEOs, she didn't try to conform to a particular leadership style or fulfill a preconceived role. Instead, she acted naturally, wearing the stylish clothes she favored; being inclusive; and displaying her natural intelligence and confidence. She took Avon in a direction that reflected who she was—she wanted the company to become more upscale, more image-conscious, more bold in its marketing. Though not everyone agreed with all of Andrea's decisions during that first year, everyone recognized that she wasn't putting on an act. Not only did this genuine quality earn her respect, but it made her stand out from other leaders. She was comfortable in her own skin, and as a result, people believed in her in a way that they might not have believed in slicker but less authentic leaders.

FOUR

THE ROYAL BRAND

2000–2004

WHILE MANY CEOS ARE GOOD LEADERS, FEW PUT THEIR PERSONAL STAMP ON A COMPANY. People such as Meg Whitman at eBay, Mark Zuckerberg at Facebook, and Steve Jobs at Apple are some well-known examples of top leaders who reshaped their organizations successfully; they're often either founders or joined their organizations in their formative stages. They had the time and the authority to implement their vision, and their vision changed the company for the better, both internally and externally.

Though Andrea was neither a founder nor an early employee of the company, she certainly belongs among this elite group. After her first year at the helm, she had the power and the platform to implement a series of programs and strategies that not only added momentum to the turnaround she initiated in her first year but made Avon a bigger and better organization. More important, she reinvented key aspects of Avon that paved the way for growth and increased profit.

Between 2000 and 2004, Andrea launched initiatives that drove margin improvement, raised Avon's global profile, expanded into the retail space, and evolved the corporate structure and culture. During this time, Andrea was highly visible and involved (except for one dormant stretch, which I'll discuss), and though not everything she tried worked, a large percentage of it did. As triumph followed triumph, Andrea's halo glowed at its brightest. She was doing what most CEOs only dream of: making the company her own and growing it profitably in the process. It was a turnaround of the highest order, and people noticed.

To understand her brilliance at leading the company during these years, we need to start with Avon's evolution as a global company, since this was a major factor in Andrea's success.

MANAGING THE GLOBAL-LOCAL CONUNDRUM

How does an organization leverage economies of scale while customizing its products and services to meet local requirements? This is the paradox that many global organizations are struggling with, and the one that confronted Andrea as she settled in as CEO. At Avon, however, numerous factors made the struggle even more challenging than for the typical organization. It's worth spending a bit of time explaining what these factors were, since it provides rich fodder for any leader trying to deal with a confounding global-local conflict.

Avon first began entering markets outside of the United States in the 1950s, starting with Venezuela and Puerto Rico to gain a foothold in Latin America, then expanding into the United Kingdom as a base for larger European operations. In the 1960s, Avon opened an office in Japan, and in 1990, it became the first major cosmetics company to manufacture and sell products in China. The company opened for business in Russia about a year later.

More so than for many organizations during this time period, global expansion was an integral strategy for Avon because of its direct-selling model. This model was tailor-made for countries less developed than the United States that lacked department stores and drug stores outside of major cities where women could purchase cosmetics. The stores that did exist in these countries often lacked the selection of products that Avon could offer. Equally important, a job as an Avon representative offered a great income opportunity for women in these areas of the world.

Because Avon entered these markets before most of their competitors, customized products to local needs, and displayed a degree of agility in their country strategies, it was enormously successful. In 2002, for instance, Latin America represented 27 percent of Avon's annual sales. Just as significant, when Andrea became CEO, the United States represented approximately 60 percent of Avon's total sales. This is what truly made Andrea's global strategy an integral part of her vision for Avon— she had to figure out how to contemporize a declining US market while simultaneously continuing to expand an overseas one.

Complicating matters, Avon was moving from a holding company model to an integrated framework—one that leveraged economies of scale and brands. Yet the transition was difficult, as each country ran their business more as a private fiefdom than as a connected part of a larger whole. To maintain margins and customer prices, for example, each country often sourced their own ingredients and didn't adhere to a common corporate standard. Consequently, quality varied considerably from country to country. The Avon logos were not even the same and packaging varied widely. Creating and enforcing global standards was the objective, but doing so would negate the local customization that had been essential for Avon's success in overseas markets—Latin American women liked sweeter-scented perfume and bolder colors for eyes and lips than US customers, and Asian women were buying skin whiteners.

As much as Andrea wanted to centralize power at the corporate level and establish a brand-centric, universal approach, she recognized that doing so could damage Avon's overseas markets. For a while, it was difficult to find the right global-local balance. But Andrea kept looking, and the breakthrough came as a result of consultant's work for Avon, in which it was suggested that Avon didn't have one market but five distinct ones at different stages of maturity. The most mature— the United States, France, the United Kingdom, etc.—had established brands, well-understood buying patterns, and a more mature customer. The least mature—the developing markets—were just starting to accumulate disposable income and focus on beauty brands for the first time.

The concept of the "5 Avons" provided the company with a common language to discuss the differences and an effective way to create a market segmentation strategy.

Still, the global-local paradox proved an ongoing leadership challenge for Andrea. There were many situations with no easy answers. In Indonesia, for instance, the country manager said that his customers couldn't afford the standard size of deodorant and wanted to manufacture a smaller size—he found that his customers would prefer to buy smaller sizes more frequently, even if it cost more in the long run. Corporate's response was to turn down the request, insisting that to leverage economies of scale, all markets needed to adopt the same size packaging. This same general manager had also been talking about offering sachets, small packets of a product that contained enough supply for one day. In the early 2000s, most people in the United States did not even know what sachets were. They ended up becoming a key part of Procter & Gamble's (P&G) offering in emerging markets. Part of the problem was that when Avon executives visited these countries, they often stayed in the largest cities and didn't receive a complete picture of a market situation. They didn't realize that in some places in South America many representatives delivered their products to customers by horseback, and in Indonesia they were often delivered by boat. It was a perfect illustration of a truism that has become very apparent since the advent of globalization: leaders don't receive a clear picture until they're on the ground—and then often not until they cover a lot of ground.

More than any other country, Brazil was an example of that truism. Brazil was a cash cow for Avon, and it would eventually become Avon's largest market, but for the average Avon executive in the United States who had spent little time in Brazil, its excellent performance would have been a mystery. It was only when you immersed yourself in the culture and spent time talking with the reps and the executives in that country in an effort to understand the country that you could grasp why Brazil represented such a terrific market for the company. While Avon may have seemed like an old-fashioned brand in the United States at the start of the twenty-first century, it was considered a hip and trendy brand in Brazil. Direct selling was embraced by the country's citizens, and the direct-selling channel was growing in double-digits; direct sellers had more market share than competitors Colgate or P&G. In many parts of the country, the US-based Avon and its English-speaking executives were esteemed—the "Yankee go home" mentality that existed in other South American countries was not prevalent in Brazil. Eventually, though, the idiosyncrasies of this market would create another challenge for Andrea and Avon, but that was in the future.

If the first challenge was the global-local paradox, the second challenge was prioritizing markets for investment. At the time, it seemed that China, Russia, Poland, and Brazil should be top priorities, while countries such as India were considered low potential. The Russian numbers were enticing, as Euromonitor International predicted that the cosmetics and toiletries market could grow between $15 billion and $18 billion annually in the next 20 years. In India, although the numbers for potential beauty growth were also large, customers appeared to be primarily from the large cities, where the primary sales channel was retail. In the outlying villages, it appeared to Andrea and others that women outside the major cities weren't sufficiently sophisticated to be good Avon customers, and so they were relegated to a low strategic priority—a mistake that only became apparent years later. Many Avon executives I interviewed insisted that there were few resources to go around and that the bets placed on Russia paid out in the long run and the investments in China should have. I'll explain later why China failed to yield the desired results.

CHINA: COMPLEXITY MULTIPLIED

In many ways, China serves as a paradigm for Andrea's leadership strengths (and eventually for her weaknesses as well). Because of Andrea's Chinese heritage, this country assumed a place of great importance in her strategy. She also recognized that though Avon had been an established seller under Jim Preston's leadership in China since 1990, it had not come close to realizing the market's potential.

When Andrea took over as CEO, Avon China had a sales team of 350,000 representatives, and the company's revenue was at $160 million with sales being projected to top $1 billion by 2010. In 1998, however, the Chinese government banned all direct selling because of entrepreneurs who were running scams or acting unethically, at least by Western business standards. Avon, though, didn't want to give up this increasingly lucrative market and decided to shift its Chinese business model to a franchise retail outlet concept that took the form of beauty boutiques. These boutiques, some of which were freestanding and some of which appeared at department store counters, supported store representatives who delivered to individual customers. This model had already enjoyed some success for Avon in Taiwan, and this was one of the reasons that Andrea brought in Avon's Taiwanese general manager, SK Kao, to run the Chinese operation. To demonstrate her commitment to the country, Andrea issued a statement that read in part, "We are in China for the long term and are rapidly building brand awareness among Chinese women." Soon, sales were back to the levels that existed before direct selling was banned, and by 2005, there were 6,000 Avon Beauty Boutiques in every province throughout China.

So while Andrea's strategy was highly successful, it also contained the seeds of its own destruction. Then and now, establishing a profitable, sustainable business in the non-Western world looks easier than it actually is. It's easy for business leaders to invest money, open stores and offices, and generate revenue. What trips leaders up is a wide range of cultural, political, and other issues waiting just beneath the surface that, if not addressed properly, can create problems—sometimes huge problems. When asked about China, a former senior leader remarked, "We were always very good at understanding the cultural differences in these markets. We never understood and underestimated the role of the Chinese government and what it takes to operate in that environment."

In China, there were several below-the-surface problems:

- Avon was embarking on a retail strategy with a direct-selling mindset. It never possessed or built retail core capabilities, such as merchandising and displays, relying instead on the boutiques to do the selling. While some of the boutiques in the major cities were solid, their quality in second- and third-tier cities was questionable at best.

- "There is no brand strategy." This is a quote from one Avon sales executive during Andrea's launch of her China strategy. Avon salespeople at the department store counters were competing with the boutiques, which were competing with other distribution channels. There was no market segmentation. But because of the double-digit growth, no one worried about the lack of a brand strategy, or at least they didn't do anything about it.

- The leadership ability of SK Kao was inconsistent. He was delivering excellent results and was an astute businessperson, but his leadership style leaned more towards intimidation and often prevented inclusion. Turnover among the younger, more assertive staff was high, as they sometimes did not feel as though their ideas were valued or even welcomed. He also brought in a group of Taiwanese executives to complete his senior staff team. The mainland Chinese employees often referred to them as the "Taiwan mafia"—a clique where others were not welcomed. The Taiwanese executives were known to be more outspoken and aggressive than the mainland Chinese, which created tensions in the organization. A number of corporate Avon executives were aware of these issues and urged Andrea to intervene, especially in light of her public declaration that how leaders got their results was just as important as the results that were achieved. She found it difficult to do so because he was meeting, or exceeding his sales targets consistently and there was no one ready to take his place. At the time, Ben Gallina was running the Asia region, and as SK's boss, even he found it difficult to coach and manage SK or even at times to get information from him. Although SK was the quintessential Avon entrepreneur, he was different from many of the country managers in that most of them displayed tremendous loyalty and were protective of Andrea. SK, however, was suspicious of outsiders interfering with his business and sometimes seemed more interested in telling corporate staff what they wanted to hear rather than what they needed to know.

Despite these problems, Andrea pursued her China strategy as if she were the leader of a nation rather than just a business. She used her charisma to great effect as she negotiated with the Chinese government to rescind their ban on direct selling. Andrea just knew that if the ban were lifted, Avon's sales would increase dramatically. She began negotiating with government officials, insisting that Avon was a highly ethical company and deserved to be one of the first organizations to resume direct sales.

Madame Wu Yi was one of the four vice premiers of the State Council at the time and the person responsible for lifting the direct-selling ban. Known as the Iron Lady and a tough negotiator, she was one of the most influential women not only in China but in the world, and she was willing to meet with Andrea when Andrea returned to China. Prior to the meeting, Andrea took several steps to increase the likelihood of success. Avon executives suspected that many of its competitors in China were not quite operating aboveboard with the Chinese government, but they also realized that Andrea needed to offer Madame Wu Yi a gift at the end of the meeting, in keeping with the Chinese tradition of gifts as a sign of respect. The company was in the midst of rolling out ethics training throughout the organization, so selecting an appropriate gift, under the prescribed price limit, was a tricky proposition requiring several meetings and numerous discussions. The gift needed to be impressive enough to show respect but not too nice that it would even hint at an impropriety. In the end, an appropriate small gift was selected. Andrea also had Avon participate in efforts by the American Chamber of Commerce, the US-China Business Council, and the World Federation of Direct Selling to lobby the Chinese government to lift the ban on direct selling.

At Avon headquarters, corporate staff were excited about the meeting. Being granted the first license for direct selling since it was forbidden would represent a huge win, not just in future revenues, but for Avon's reputation in foreign markets. The meeting with Madame Wu Yi, which happened with a translator, even though Andrea was fluent in Mandarin, went extremely well—they both believed in women's empowerment, and this common bond helped things go smoothly. There were subsequent meetings with Madame Wu Yi and her colleagues, and in 2005, the Chinese government, much to the dismay of competitors, approved Avon to proceed with a limited test of direct selling in the cities of Beijing and Tianjin. Andrea's success in the negotiations can be attributed to many factors—her Chinese heritage, her passion and commitment to China as a key Avon market, her participation in lobbying efforts—but what stands out is that Andrea was negotiating with Madame Wu Yi as an equal. She carried herself with great dignity and authority, and this carried great weight with the Chinese government officials. They viewed her as American royalty, and this perception was evident when Andrea visited China in 2004. The Chinese team members preparing for her visit knew that Andrea's mother had emigrated from Shanghai, and they decided to locate the house where she had lived. When they found it, they found several families living there and that the home was in need of significant repair. Prior to Andrea's visit, they sent these families on "vacation" and then cleaned, painted, and repaired the house so it would be in pristine condition when they took Andrea there. Andrea never knew about this, but it was the sort of effort people usually make for a visiting dignitary, not for a corporate CEO.

RETAIL: GOING WHERE DIRECT SELLERS FEARED TO TREAD

Retail strategies had tempted Avon for years. To reach new, more, and younger customers, especially in the stagnant US market, retail held tremendous promise. Yet it also held perils. As you might imagine, Avon's management had always worried that a major retail venture would alienate representatives and cause channel conflict—if you could buy Avon products in stores, the reps were effectively cut out of the picture, or at least they were likely to perceive it that way.

Whether to make a major push into retail is a tough leadership call. Some leaders of direct-selling organizations refuse to make it, sticking with traditional strategies and ignoring opportunities. Others take the opposite approach, focused on reinventing the organization for greater glory (the company's and their own) regardless of the risk.

Though the retail strategy never ultimately succeeded in the way that Andrea envisioned, she went about it analytically, gradually and with a balanced perspective. Just as she was able to think globally and locally simultaneously, she was also able to consider the retail/direct-selling dilemma objectively and with a good understanding of both selling approaches. More than that, she embarked on her retail strategy authentically. Andrea often said, "The brand is bigger than the channel," and she crafted a retail approach designed to elevate the Avon brand. This is what she believed in, and for a while, her fervent belief carried others along and buoyed Avon through an extraordinarily difficult transition.

With US sales stagnant and Avon enjoying some success testing retail strategies in countries such as Taiwan and Malaysia, Andrea was emboldened to push her retail agenda forward. When Andrea first joined Avon, the company had launched an initiative called Complimentary Access that was designed to help them reach new and younger customers (ages 30–40); these were individuals unlikely to buy beauty products from a representative and more likely to buy them at a mall.

As part of this initiative, Avon launched a mall kiosk experiment in 1998 to sell Avon products. Customers were given the option of buying products at the kiosks or linking with an Avon representative; this alternative helped mitigate the conflict between the two distribution channels. The experiment was successful on a number of fronts, but the big news was that 90–95 percent of the buyers were new to Avon. Conceivably, then, retail might help drive the growth strategy that Andrea envisioned. Andrea conducted further studies that favored organic growth over acquisitions and recommended a partnership to fuel this growth.

As Andrea became increasingly serious about making a major retail push, she recognized that Avon lacked strong internal retail expertise and went outside the company to hire Steve Bock, one of the world's top retailing experts who had worked previously at Sephora, Saks Fifth Avenue, and with Andrea at I. Magnin. Steve was charged with considering three classes of partners: the upper class (the May Group, which included at the time stores such as Robinsons-May, Marshall Fields, and Lord & Taylor), the middle class (Sears, JC Penney), and the lower class (Walmart, Target). He and Andrea quickly eliminated the upper class as being too far removed from Avon's core customer and the lower class as being too supply-chain focused, which was outside of Avon's core capabilities, as well as duplicating Avon's customer base and creating a conflict between the two distribution channels.

They forged an alliance with JC Penney and Sears and in late 2000 began to work on turning Andrea's retail vision into reality. While they came to a formal agreement with both chains, Sears was seen as the key to a successful launch. Inside each Sears store would be an Avon retail space, occupying about 600 feet and selling a completely new, premium brand separate from Avon's regular line of products. No expense was spared as Steve and Andrea hired the best designers, merchandisers, and retail consultants. Almost $100 million (some of which came from Avon and some from the partner companies) was budgeted for the startup. The store designs were stunning, even futuristic. It soon became clear that Andrea saw these stores as more than mere sellers of premium merchandise; she envisioned them as gathering places for women to receive information about beauty as well as other subjects. In fact, it was even floated by Andrea that Avon might purchase or partner with a financial services firm.

Unlike many leaders obsessed by their vision and oblivious to everything else, Andrea was sensitive to the ramifications of this retail move, especially the risk of offending Avon's representatives. First, she made sure the products were different from the ones that the representatives sold; the retail products were also priced higher. Organizationally, Andrea made a point to separate the retail group's processes, compensation, and other functions so as not to create internal competition for the core business. Even the product development process for retail was different and much faster—it took only nine months from concept to production.

The company launched their retail group with a splash. This was Andrea's strength, and she managed to generate a great deal of fanfare and media coverage. To an outsider, Andrea appeared to be once again leading Avon to greater growth and profit with her charismatic style. But insiders knew there were two major problems with this retail strategy.

First, partnering with Sears and JC Penney was risky. Though their customers were a notch above those of a retailer like Walmart, they also overlapped with the traditional Avon customer. If the goal was to attract a new, younger, more upscale customer, these partners might not be in the best position to help. Second, a significant number of Avon executives didn't back the retail initiative—they thought it would take the company away from its direct-selling roots.

Then Sears pulled out of the partnership before it even began. Sears Chairman and CEO Alan Lacy issued a statement that said, in part, "Sears now sees a diminished role for cosmetics in the future positioning of its full-line stores. We fully understand that this is inconsistent with Avon's desired position for its new brand and that it is no longer appropriate to move forward together on this initiative."[1] Though Sears compensated Avon handsomely (around $20 million) for ending the relationship, it was a major blow. Andrea being Andrea, however, she moved forward without missing a beat. Her enthusiasm remained high, and she focused on rolling out the Avon centers in JC Penney with a new line that included skin care, color cosmetics, a line for new moms, post-exercise products, and perfumes.

By early 2003, however, the retail experiment was over. Andrea admitted that the company could not get up to the scale needed to drive a long term, viable business with just internal resources. "It was probably the wrong partner," she said. "If we did it again, we would do something longer and put in more resources over a longer period of time."[2] Despite pulling the plug, Andrea didn't admit that retail was dead for Avon. In fact, she reiterated that the company would continue to pursue retail opportunities, and acquisitions were discussed. She also retained Steve Bock, the retail head. Yet nothing happened on the acquisition front, and a few months after Andrea announced that Steve would stay on, he left the company.

It was a setback, but it didn't deter Andrea from forging ahead with other initiatives. She is quoted as saying about the failed retail venture, "I'm still glad we did it. I think we learned a lot."[3] The faith she had in her vision and her ability to put a positive spin on a setback was undiminished. Leaders who can rally the troops and maintain a consistent message tend to succeed despite what fate and competitors throw at them, and Andrea could do both as well as anyone.

GETTING BACK UP ON THE HORSE

Some leaders get gun-shy after a public failure and play it safe. Not Andrea. She embarked on two growth strategies that were just as bold as the retail initiative, if not quite as expensive. They were also aligned with her vision of Avon as a company for a younger, more stylish, and more upscale clientele.

The first, mark., began when she brought in Debi Fine. Debi, a marketing and public relations expert who was especially skilled at selling to younger people, was put in charge of the new division. Andrea's thinking was that a new Avon division with separate products designed for women ages 16 to 25 would not only bolster a weak demographic for Avon but provide this group with an income-generating opportunity and allow them to discover Avon much as their mothers and grandmothers had done. The tag line of mark. was, "Make money, make friends, make a difference, make your mark." It was a sophisticated strategy, and young representatives who signed on early were also given the opportunity to earn college credits through the University of Phoenix. Debi did her job well, and Avon made another big media splash—for months you couldn't open a magazine or turn on the television without seeing mark. mentioned. By the end of 2003, Avon's mark. group had more than 300 products and 20,000 sales representatives. Andrea's larger vision was to take mark. global just as Avon had translated other concepts to overseas markets. But in the end it came up short. It's not clear if mark. was a flawed strategy, a solid strategy that was poorly executed or an initiative with unrealistic expectations. It was forecasted to achieve $100 million in sales in 2004, but mark.'s actual sales were approximately $47 million. Although some countries, especially the United Kingdom, were anxious to explore the product and sales model further, expansion plans were put on hold. Debi left the company in 2005.

At the same time, Avon was also implementing another growth strategy. In 2001, Andrea made a deal with Roche to provide Avon with vitamins and supplements, and this was the start of the company's Health and Wellness group. Again, this wasn't just another product line but a new business focused on nutrition, weight management, fitness, (structured as a partnership with the health club company Curves) and a new line, Planet Spa. Susan had predicted that it could be a $1 billion business in the future. Like mark., Health and Wellness got off to a great start publicity-wise, with a goal of between $200 and $300 million in sales over the next five years and a US launch followed by a rollout to 15 foreign markets.

So the Avon renaissance was well under way, despite the retail hiccup and the new initiatives not quite fulfilling their potential. Brand recognition and brand quality had increased, the US market had picked up momentum, overseas markets were continuing to grow, and operating margin had increased. Andrea was still surrounded by her aura of greatness.

Andrea's ability to generate tremendous optimism and support within Avon and outside the company was astonishing. More than that, it helped create the company's remarkable gains during this period. Andrea had an almost sixth sense about when and how to talk about the next big thing. And there was always something new, something to rally the troops around. She could speak to one person or thousands and generate excitement about, and commitment to, whatever had seized her interest—a new line of lipsticks or an innovative technology for manufacturing products or a bold initiative in foreign markets. Her force of personality combined with her eloquence of expression to sway whatever audience she was addressing,

It wasn't just her words but her sense of when to use an emotional, theatrical appeal. At Avon's large sales rep meetings, especially, she would close with a film that would tug at the heartstrings. At one meeting, Andrea was crying in response to the uplifting message coming across on the screen; many in the audience joined her with their own tears. While she may have used this technique too often, it was clearly effective, and for every cynical audience member who thought she was being manipulative, there were a hundred others who were inspired by her.

Andrea was astute about maintaining her aura. For instance, she bent over backward not to be the one to deliver bad news. If an individual had to be reprimanded, she would hand that task off to someone else. She also relied on three excellent coaches during these years. She was always asking them for honest feedback (though at times they may have been reluctant to provide her with the pure, unadulterated truth). Nonetheless, she was eager to learn and improve as a leader, and these coaches facilitated her growth. For the five or six golden years as CEO, she rarely made the sort of gaffe that can tarnish a leader's image, and this was due in part to her willingness to listen and learn.

In the previous chapter, I noted how Andrea's vulnerability made her people protective of and loyal to her, and she continued to display behaviors that endeared her to employees and counteracted her occasional aloofness. For instance, at a company outing, one of the activities was horseback riding. Though this wasn't something that Andrea knew how to do, she went riding with everyone else (in her Chanel flats), and it communicated her willingness to leave the inner sanctum of the company and be a regular gal. Her frequent conversations about the importance of family and being a good mom reinforced this image.

Andrea's aura extended beyond the analysts, the media, and her employees to the Avon board. A colleague of Andrea's referred to the Andrea-board relationship as a "love fest," which is an apt description. Part of this was because they were awestruck by how she had led the company's turnaround. Part of it, though, was because Andrea orchestrated the board meetings so that she came out smelling like roses. On more than one occasion, she and her people storyboarded presentations to the board beforehand, as if they were putting together a shooting script for a television commercial. She sequenced messages so that if there was bad news to deliver, it would come right after she announced some piece of positive news—the good would obscure the bad. In one instance, concerned that the board might question her about a lack of a successor, she made a presentation on all the great new talent the company had brought in. Impressed, the board didn't push her on a successor.

Certainly Andrea's beauty, intellectual brilliance, and dramatic style helped create the halo that hovered perpetually over her head. But she also helped craft her image, and it helped her become a leader who seemingly could do no wrong.

Andrea's aura took her and the company far, but there were other, more substantive cultural and leadership challenges that she needed to address in order to facilitate even more growth and profitability.

THE IMPACT OF A LEADER ON THE CULTURE

To a certain extent, all CEOs who hold the position for a sufficiently long period of time have an impact on their cultures. By definition, a CEO's style is reflected back in the culture—most managers' work behaviors mirror the big boss's, at least to some extent. At GE, there were a lot of midlevel managerial versions of Jack Welch; likewise at Apple under Steve Jobs. This is a natural process, but what Andrea attempted to do was change the culture from the top down, to create new leadership competencies that would reward new cultural behaviors foreign to the old Avon. Trying to change a culture in this way—especially one as solidly established as Avon's—is a significant leadership task. Let's look at how Andrea went about it.

First, this story illustrates how entrenched Avon's cultural problems were. In 2003, a consulting firm provided recommendations to help Avon's cultural evolution that bore a distinct similarity to another consultant's report—from 1991! The report said that teams at Avon tended to submerge differences and avoid conflict, jump to conclusions, cast blame, and be overly protective during problem-solving and decision-making situations. The consultant also noted that when setting goals, people were often vague and soft (in terms of holding people accountable for achieving goals). The 2003 consultant's report suggested that people at Avon needed to be more candid during their interactions with each other and rely more on analysis during problem solving. It also found that they had to drive hard to resolve problems. The report recommended setting clearer priorities and reducing the number of initiatives on which the organization was working.

Just as the culture was in need of change, so too was the leadership model. I had worked with Andrea and her senior team to construct this model early in her tenure, and during the construction, we identified key leadership competencies. Yet I noticed that Andrea never referred to this model when she spoke about leadership and seemed not to value the standard competencies related to developing people, customer focus, and so on. Though Andrea and her senior team were aware of, and had signed off on, the competencies in the model, they had never really owned or internalized them. One day I decided to confront her about this. She discussed the qualities that were important to her—a significantly different set from those in the model. We called in Susan Kropf, got out our pens, and began listing the leadership traits that would drive the next phase of growth. They included the following:

PASSIONATE DRIVER

- Has a relentless accountability for results
- Has the courage to make the tough calls

GLOBAL BUILDER

- Is a strategic thinker and action-oriented implementer
- Thrives on diversity of perspectives

TALENT NURTURER

- Puts the right people in the right jobs
- Differentiates performance

EMOTIONALLY INTELLIGENT

- Strives for self-awareness
- Is upfront and candid

Once we had identified these qualities, we incorporated them into 360-degree feedback instruments and a second round of leadership development and alignment programs. Perhaps even more important, Andrea took ownership of the new model. You knew when Andrea believed in something because she talked about it consistently and passionately. In one-on-one conversations as well as more formal external and internal talks, Andrea promoted these leadership qualities, and it had a significant impact on people's work behaviors.

LOCO GLOBAL: A CRAZY-MAKING TASK

Brilliant men and women have written a gazillion words about global leadership. Yet the specific issues facing global organizations remain so ambiguous, paradoxical, complicated, and volatile that any theory or advice is eventually ineffective.

Implementing Andrea's global vision was an ever-daunting, ever-evolving task. Earlier we saw how Avon faced a local-global paradox that required a delicate balancing of locally tailored programs with corporate-wide initiatives. Complicating matters, Avon's direct-selling model took different forms in different countries. Avon had a long history of doing things certain ways in certain countries, and it was attempting to change the decision-making structure—moving from a model where country heads were basically in charge of everything to one where they were more like sales managers who relied on regional and corporate executives for other functional programs and decisions. Clustered countries in specific regions would collaborate and establish regional control over manufacturing, marketing, and so on. As you can imagine, the general managers in these countries were rankled by the reduction in their responsibilities—they now had to defer to the head of marketing for whatever regional cluster they belonged to. We were fortunate at the time that the European organization had already migrated to more of a cluster configuration as a strategy to drive their global expansion, so there were already many converts and best practices from which to draw.

Inevitably, the reorganization created a complex set of matrix reporting relationships. Corporate, regional, and country senior executives were involved in the decision-making process, but it was often unclear who had the final say over certain decisions. In many instances, when confusion occurred or an impasse was reached, the executives involved would cry for Mom/Andrea to be the arbitrator. Though her response was invariably that she wanted the parties in conflict to resolve matters themselves, they often weren't able to do so.

We brought in Ram Charan, one of the world's leading consultants, to help us develop a program that would allow people around the world to work more effectively within a matrix structure. He emphasized the importance of clarifying who was responsible for deciding what, and we spent many hours in conference rooms with flip charts trying to identify where roles overlapped. While we achieved clarity in the conference room, this consensus broke down in the field as people assumed more decision-making control than was appropriate. We had all agreed that if people overstepped their roles, there would be consequences. Unfortunately, Avon's culture of politeness prevented these consequences from actually taking place. Too often, these managers escaped punishment, which ended up reinforcing these counterproductive behaviors. In some instances, when leaders played out of position, even Andrea failed to call out the bad behavior or hold leaders accountable for their actions—another example of her occasional "blinking."

Despite Ram Charan's excellent work and Avon's internal controls, this problem wasn't solved until 2005, when marketing and supply chain processes were globalized and the transformation team and new roles and responsibilities were finally clarified. The power of Avon's culture and multiple forms of resistance cannot be underestimated. Powerful leaders often feel they can change cultures, and while they may be able to make some significant changes, certain ingrained elements, especially in a 100-plus-year-old company, are difficult to dislodge. If any CEO possessed a mandate and the credibility to change a culture, Andrea did. Yet there was always some cultural norm that would assert itself and hamper implementation of a new program or policy. In a relationship-based culture lacking strong business discipline and processes such as Avon's, things typically get done through the know-how of an individual manager and this manager's reliance on key people who also understand how to execute. This culture was powerful and had been highly effective for years. To change it—and change it quickly—was a huge undertaking.

Andrea, too, probably didn't demonstrate the full commitment to remaking the culture from top to bottom that she might have. She focused much more on the top than anywhere else—perhaps believing that the top would catalyze and cascade the change. In the case of changing global decision-making responsibilities, the cultural response took the form of regional groups building up their staffs at the same time that corporate was expanding their groups. Different groups were bulking up in order to gain greater control over their turf. This is a natural occurrence as an organization moves to become more globally integrated, because the operating mechanisms required demand tremendous resources and coordination. While Andrea's efforts did bring in a number of world-class marketing and supply chain staff, they also created an unsustainable cost structure. In a tougher culture, this expansion would most likely not have been tolerated or would at least have been monitored more closely.

THE GOLDEN AGE IN PERSPECTIVE

In hindsight, Avon was in its glory from 2001 until 2004. Even Andrea looks upon these years as the good old days. Despite the global issues and the retail problems, Avon truly became the Company for Women, an organization with a larger global market, a more diverse product line, and a more appealing, stylish image. This transformation paid dividends, and in a keynote address at the 2003 Conference Board, Andrea enumerated these dividends to a packed conference room:

- The best stock return to its shareholders in its history.
- A stock price increase of 63 percent from 2000 to 2002.
- Expansion in the field to more than 3.9 million Avon representatives worldwide.
- Double-digit growth in its markets.
- Avon regularly listed as one of the world's best-managed companies.
- Expansion of the Avon Foundation.

It's worth noting that, despite Avon's great growth and success and all the accolades Andrea received, she remained humble. Arrogance or hubris is the biggest trap for highly successful leaders, and Andrea adroitly sidestepped it. When book publishers approached Andrea to write about herself and the remarkable turnaround of Avon, she declined. Partly, she didn't want to raise expectations for the company to unrealistic levels with a book. Mainly, though, she always put the company before herself. Though she was charismatic and dynamic and loved to present her vision to the world, she managed her ego well. This allowed her to focus all her energy on strategies for growth, and most of the ones she introduced during this golden age—wellness, teens, overseas markets—paid off.

In this golden age, it was impossible to imagine that seemingly minor glitches and setbacks would turn into huge problems within the next few years. The retail debacle, major growth initiatives that in the end never achieved the forecasted potential, the increasingly bloated staffs, and the global-local confusion appeared to be minor irritants rather than fatal flaws. Given this perception, no one at Avon or outsider observers of the company could anticipate that Andrea would soon be leading the company out of a golden age into a full-blown crisis.

LEADERSHIP LESSONS LEARNED

1. *Keep new businesses separate when culture clashes and other types of dissonance are likely.* Andrea introduced a number of new businesses to Avon in a short amount of time. Wisely, she kept them separate from Avon's core business, insisting that each have its own budgetary, compensation, and other processes. In addition, she didn't try to transfer managers from Avon's main business to the new businesses; she brought in world-class outside experts to ensure that people with the right knowledge and skills would be in charge. She also made sure that the new businesses' cultures wouldn't clash with Avon's direct-selling culture. It's common for leaders to fail to see the value of separation. Kodak made this mistake when it tried to have its digital business coexist with its traditional film business.

2. *Communicate, communicate, and communicate some more.* Andrea was especially good at getting her points across clearly, compellingly, and consistently to the top two layers of management. While she wasn't as good with people below these levels, her ability to get key people on board for her initiatives was critical. Given the number of new programs and strategies she introduced, it was essential that people "get it" and "own it." With her inclusive one-on-one style and her motivational speaking skill, Andrea got her points across better than most leaders. As a result, there were very few slipups in implementation, because everyone understood what was required, and they bought in to the initiatives.

3. *Acknowledge and adjust to global-local complexities.* The biggest mistake leaders make is trying to find simple solutions to problems that can't be solved. Andrea was situational and flexible when confronted by the need to create consistent quality and

image globally and the need to tailor products and other programs to local markets. The concept of managing these paradoxes (global and local, customized and unique) became an issue during this time period, and Andrea and her team were adroit at finding a good balance between two seemingly opposite positions. She seemed to find the right balance in places such as China and Latin America. As focused as she was on brand, she knew when to sacrifice the brand in some instances to ensure that a given country could meet the particular needs of its market.

4. *Use failure as an incentive to succeed.* It is human instinct to play it safe after making a major, public mistake. Even though the retail initiative at Avon didn't succeed as Andrea had hoped, she didn't let it stop her from implementing other initiatives that also carried a degree of risk—mark. and Health and Wellness. It was almost as if she had a chip on her shoulder and declared, "I'll show them!" She launched these new groups with boldness, ensuring that their success or failure would be seen by everyone. Using failure as an incentive is easy advice to give and tough advice to follow. But good leaders possess sufficient confidence to risk bad luck scuttling their efforts again, believing in their abilities and companies sufficiently that they continue to take risks and introduce new concepts.

5. *Don't forget the power of the culture.* To Andrea's credit, she recognized this power by devoting considerable time and effort to recreating the leadership qualities that she prized in her people. When confronted with the fact that Avon's current leadership model didn't focus on these qualities, she worked with her people to create a new model that had a positive impact on the culture. At the same time, Andrea probably

could have done a lot more to drive the culture change, and her inability to do more eventually came back to bite her. Admittedly, culture change is tricky and difficult, especially when you're dealing with an organization that has a long history and a culture over a hundred years in the making. That culture, though, can thwart even the best strategies, and in the long run it thwarted Andrea's vision.

FIVE

BEING ABLE TO FIRE HERSELF

2005–2008

MOST CEOS WHO STAY WITH THEIR ORGANIZATIONS FOR ANY EXTENDED PERIOD OF TIME will face at least one major financial downturn. It may stem from increased competition, internal problems, or just a slumping economy, but regardless, it tests a leader's resolve and abilities. Some leaders can't stand the pressure and resign. Others become conservative and play it safe, trusting that their existing strategy, as well as external events, will help them turn things around.

Andrea, though, chose a different path. In 2005, Avon missed its first earnings forecast since she took over as CEO. While others in the company were anxious, Andrea remained optimistic and made an aggressive next quarter estimate, convinced that the bad quarter was an anomaly. But they missed the next quarter's estimate again, and the stock price fell 45 percent between April and October 2005. During this period, the quarterly analyst meeting took place that became known internally as the "mea culpa" meeting. At the meeting, Andrea admitted that a long list of things were broken in the business, including employee bloat (too many people doing too little work), increasing product SKUs that were driving up costs without providing the requisite value, a product discount rate of 80 percent (versus 65 percent

in previous years), and competitors chipping away at market share everywhere except Brazil. Andrea also confessed that, although the business had been growing, it was not in a sustainable way—it was more
through muscle and pure resolve. She recognized that some of the core
businesses processes were not in place to guarantee continued growth.

Like all great leaders, Andrea was reenergized by these difficult
situations. Rather than leave or play it safe, she embarked on a bold
course of action. Andrea had never failed before, and she wasn't going
to start now. She did the hardest thing a leader is called upon to do:
admit that the way you've been running the business is no longer effective and that you have to change direction if you want to be successful.
It takes humility, brains, and guts to make this admission, and Andrea
demonstrated she had all three in spades. What she lacked, though, was
a willingness to displease people. Not many pleasers become CEOs,
in part because the path to the top job requires that they put the business first. Invariably, they must make choices that hurt the people they
manage—downsizing, for instance. That Andrea made it to the top
despite her desire to please others is remarkable—it's a testament to
her marketing skills, her charisma, and her vision. This time, she would
have to get tough, move fast, and make some difficult decisions. Ultimately, however, it seems she stopped short of doing many of the painful things necessary to right the ship for the long haul.

THE ILLUSION OF EVERLASTING SUCCESS

Between 1999 and 2004, Avon experienced unprecedented overseas
growth, product and image transformation, and changes to its operational model that helped set it on a profitable path. Andrea and Avon
were the darlings of Wall Street, and their prospects seemed bright. Yet
after a 181 percent rise in the stock price since Andrea's appointment,
that price fell to $25 per share in the final months of 2005, coming up
short of Wall Street and the board's expectations. As successful as her
growth strategy had been, many of the new initiatives weren't doing

as well as everyone had hoped, and the image-related decision to stop stocking nonbeauty items had hurt sales in some markets. More important, overstaffing in response to the global-local conundrum had led to increased overhead and confused decision making. Combined with struggling overseas markets and a culture that was not as accountable and performance-driven as it should have been, the company was ill-prepared for an increasingly global, competitive environment. A consultant's report at the time spotlighted four problem areas:

- A lack of fact-based decision making
- Various country heads still possessing more power than the central organization
- Indecisiveness—decisions were made and then unmade because of poorly defined processes, unclear lines of authority, and at times, a passive-resistant culture
- The absence of a plan to create an organizational structure aligned with Avon's future objectives and growth

Interestingly, this same consultant also noted the need to preserve certain aspects of Avon's culture and operations. First, the report commented on the unusually deep connection employees had with Avon: like the company itself and its direct-selling model, relationships came first with the employees. Second, the report praised Avon's entrepreneurial spirit and the way each group in each country found ways to make their numbers regardless of fluctuating economies or currencies—the innovative approach to sales was a remarkable, ongoing achievement.

The challenge for Andrea, therefore, was maintaining these defining, profitable traits while addressing the problems besetting the company. Logically, if she were to take a significant amount of power away from the country heads, they might lose their entrepreneurial spirit. If she were to toughen up the company's culture and push people harder for results, the connection employees felt to the company might dissolve. These were, in many ways, the same challenges she had faced in her first four years on the job. Although the organization had made progress, Andrea often commented internally that, "We often take two steps forward and one step back. It's still not enough."

ANDREA HAD ALWAYS SEEN HERSELF as a growth-oriented, marketing-focused executive, but the company needed a different type of CEO at this point. It took a good deal of soul searching, but Andrea finally accepted reality and resolved to be this new type of CEO.

A conversation with consultant Ram Charan fostered this epiphany. Ram had been working with Andrea and the organization off and on for years and knew both her and the situation well. When she came to him asking for assistance, he told her, "Look, they [the board, the employees, the media, the analysts] love you. Everyone wants you to win, but if you can't fire yourself [on Friday] . . . and come back on Monday morning . . . [You were] put in the job to do a turnaround and do all the objective things that somebody with fresh eyes can. . . . If you can't do that, this is going to be a tough haul."[1]

Maybe it was the way Ram phrased his advice, or maybe Andrea was just in a place to take it to heart. Whatever the reason, she fully embraced the "fire yourself" lesson. Seemingly overnight, Andrea became a different type of leader—the Turnaround Queen. Just as her growth/marketing focus fit Avon well until 2005, her new leadership persona was equally effective after that year. Andrea had to work against her grain: she had to downsize and delay and cut costs and programs that had been her babies. It could not have been easy; she even managed a certain amount of displeasing of others to implement these changes. Eventually, Ram's "fire yourself" advice became her mantra in speeches and media interviews. She convinced herself of its truth by convincing others. She recognized that some things can't be delegated, that it was up to her to deliver the tough messages.

With the zeal of a politician running for reelection, she took to the stump. She launched a barnstorming world tour in which she held town halls with employees at all levels, explaining the why and how of the new order. As you might imagine, her messages of cuts and accountability created organization-wide anxiety. But it was necessary. She was aware of her reputation for shying away from the tough calls, and she wanted to send a message that she was stepping up. At the same time, her directness and willingness to talk to anyone and everyone about the implications of the message helped people accept it. Andrea had built a great deal of trust equity among all segments of the organization, and drew on it even as she took her tough stance.

CUTS, TRANSFUSIONS, AND OPERATIONS

During Andrea's first five years as CEO, the senior management team experienced little change. In fact, they functioned extremely well together, enjoying an unusual level of trust and cohesion for the stress-filled executive suite. While there was friendly competition (for Andrea's approval), each senior leader knew his or her role and supported the other members of the team.

But the senior team reached the same inflection point, in 2005, as the company itself. After the early financial setbacks that year, and some impending retirements, the board pushed Andrea to bring in new people with more expertise in disciplined, integrated global processes. Ideally, they wanted her to find accomplished executives from large consumer packaged-goods companies. To this end, the board prompted Andrea to select Chuck Cramb from Gillette as CFO. Chuck was a seasoned CFO whom the board thought would get expenses under control, continue to build global finance capabilities, and most important, push back against Andrea to ensure more realistic forecasts. The board had also been urging Andrea to hire a potential CEO successor, and Andrea finally responded by hiring Kraft CEO Irene Rosenfeld's protégée, Liz Smith, who came armed with sorely needed analytics skills and a reputation for execution. In addition, Lucien Alziari, the new head of HR from PepsiCo, brought an

integrated global focus to talent, and Geralyn Breig, who came from
Godiva as senior vice president/global branding, brought a consistent
approach to branding. These individuals helped reenergize not only
the business but Andrea as well.

She would need that energy, because Avon was facing rising fixed
costs and a number of struggling key markets. They had no choice but
to de-layer and reorganize, and the board hired the Boston Consulting Group to help the company start the process. In a relatively short
period of time, Andrea and her team eliminated 25 percent of management positions, reduced the managerial layers from 15 to 8 and
reduced costs dramatically, saving almost $250 million. As painful as
these actions must have been for Andrea, she knew they were essential.
Cost cutting, though, often has an unseen price, and in this instance, it
was the loss of veteran talent with an intimate understanding of direct
selling, as well as other long-term staff such as the VP of treasury, Den-
nis Ling, who had received numerous internal awards for his foreign
currency hedging and tax rate prowess (in 2002 he and his team created foreign exchange gains of $28 million).

As important as these moves were, integration was even more essential for Avon's future. Though the company had made occasional
stabs at integrating global processes, these initiatives relied largely on
individual knowledge, influence, and relationships and so were often in
favor of local interests. Over time, Avon had struggled with 40 different
methods of new product development. This is where new leaders like
Liz Smith and Geralyn Breig played crucial roles, because they knew
how to drive globalization of the new product development process
and did so zealously. They introduced a standard method, with uni-
form time lines, stage gates, and so on, equivalent to what most large,
global consumer-packaged goods companies already had.

Some of the new programs and policies dismayed veteran executives. The call for more fact-based decision making and less intuitive
choices created consternation, especially when it came to eliminating
products with lower profitability or not providing as many customer

discounts (based on product life-cycle analysis). Liz had told Andrea point-blank that she could not make the changes Andrea had hired her to implement unless she had the analytics. And although Avon had built up a large, state-of-the-art analytics group in the mid 1980s, it was disbanded in the later, lean years. Avon had enormous amounts of raw data but not the sophisticated data-mining techniques and technology to calculate marketing mix, brochure page investments, and advertising ROI that their competitors did. Consequently, Andrea gave Liz Smith the power to create a much stronger unit to facilitate fact-based decisions, and her multimillion dollar analytics group was the result. Liz successfully applied these tools in the US business, gaining credibility in the organization and convincing some of the skeptical veteran employees that this fact-based approach was viable. Similarly, Geralyn Breig was instructed by Andrea to elevate the brand, and she did so by partnering with high-end designers like Cynthia Rowley and Christian Lacroix for perfume and makeup products.

These were tough calls for Andrea, ones she had largely avoided earlier. But great leaders don't just grow businesses; they grow themselves. As much as Andrea wanted to avoid being the bad guy, she made some difficult, unpopular calls. At the end of 2005, she reorganized the company into six commercial business units and named Liz Smith as president in 2007, one year after Susan Kropf retired (though overseas markets did not report to Liz). She also centralized functions such as global product marketing and supply chain which reported to Liz.

Even more difficult for Andrea, perhaps, was enacting policies that prevented leaders from hoarding talent. Before the consolidation of talent and people processes, leaders in various departments and countries developed their own people for their groups. No longer. The company started developing people for the enterprise, moving them around the globe to help them acquire new skills as well as broader corporate understanding. Some would argue, however, that moves occurred too quickly, without individuals having time to see their strategies unfold or experience a cycle of success.

Andrea also gave up her flirtation with retail. Again, this move represented a major shift in her thinking—a shift not every leader is able to make. Retail had been an integral part of Andrea's original vision for the company. Yet by 2005, she had reaffirmed her commitment to the direct-selling model instead. This commitment meant reducing the ordering inefficiencies and other problems that made representatives less effective than they should have been. She also standardized best practices in recruiting, training, and retaining representatives and launched programs to help representatives use Internet and mobile phone applications. All this signaled that Andrea now recognized a hard truth: the business rose or fell on the number of active representatives and the size of their orders. Trying to evolve a retail component alongside this traditional model no longer seemed like the silver bullet for growth.

When Andrea assumed the CEO role, she needed to figure out how to provide competitive earnings opportunities for the representatives so they would stay with the company and be motivated to sell more. This issue was easier to put on the back burner when the company was doing well, but as things were going south, it could no longer be ignored. When Avon was founded, representatives sold to individual customers, for which they received financial incentives, discounts on products, and travel opportunities among other perks.

Because Avon didn't want to become an Amway-like pyramid system, they developed what became known as the Sales Leadership program. Essentially, it was a similar multilevel payment model now used by many direct-selling organizations, and it offered women the opportunity to make money not only by selling products but also by recruiting and training other representatives, but with a key difference in that there was a restriction on the number of levels in her sales unit.

Initially, Avon extended this multilevel model as an option in overseas markets as well. To many of the general managers in these countries, the model sounded good in theory, but didn't work in practice. It added cost to already tight budgets and was difficult to implement from a change management point of view. In addition, top-selling representatives were happy with the existing incentives and could figure out their own ways of maximizing their earnings potential. But as the need for change became more apparent with increased competition for representatives, Andrea and her team pushed this sales approach even more aggressively in the United States as well as China and other large markets despite continued protests, due to the increased cost onto their SG&A (selling, general and administrative) expenses and with only mixed results.

NEW CHINA STRATEGY

Part of the challenge of global leadership is recognizing that you're not in Kansas anymore. CEOs of global enterprises may feel they understand markets such as Russia, India, or China, since they've been there, studied the data, and talked to their top people in those countries frequently. Yet there are cultural, economic, and political nuances to doing business in these parts of the world that Westerners often don't grasp or at least give enough weight to.

Andrea certainly "got" China in many ways. As a Chinese-American and a frequent visitor to the country, she had a good sense of the market and Avon's business there. She had orchestrated a successful hybrid (retail/direct selling) strategy, establishing a track record and strong relationships there.

As previously mentioned, Andrea had made the conscious choice to wage a very high-profile, public campaign to have the Chinese government grant Avon the first direct-selling license. Given the potential of the Chinese beauty market and the growth of its direct-selling channel, the move made sense. Conversely, her single-minded focus on getting this license may have prevented her from seeing the big picture, especially the traps lurking at the edges of her vision.

In 2005, after Avon got permission to do a limited test of direct selling in Beijing and Tianjin, they ran into the challenge of how to deal with their retail outlets—the 5,500 beauty boutique owners. Many beauty boutique owners were uncertain how their future earnings would be affected now that they would now have to deal with direct-selling competitors from their own organization.

Avon recognized the need to create a change management strategy to help these owners transition to a new selling environment and made a number of efforts to make the transition as seamless as possible. For example, numerous meetings with beauty boutique owners were held and question-and-answer documents were distributed. To make matters even more awkward, the China operation had started out as a direct-selling organization and had transitioned to a retail organization, so it would now have to transition once again to a direct-selling operation.

Andrea monitored the situation closely, making frequent trips to China. In fact, during one of these trips, Andrea attended a focus group with the beauty boutique owners, and based on their comments, they appeared to be on board with the move to direct selling. Little did Andrea know that only positively inclined focus group participants were chosen. Avon's Chinese executives didn't want Andrea to be disappointed or think that the owners weren't behind the change. Culturally, they believed they had to do everything possible to make their leader happy. So they handpicked attendees to ensure a positive response and communicate the message that all was on track.

While 2005 was a transitional year for Avon in China—revenues decreased by 16 percent in the fourth quarter alone—the following year they were granted a full direct-selling license, resulting in 3 percent growth. In 2007, it appeared as if Avon had achieved a major breakthrough in the Chinese market as revenues increased 32 percent; they increased another 25 percent in 2008.

But great numbers can hide painful truths from leaders, as Avon's rebounding results between 2006 and 2008 almost certainly did. Such banner results made the competitive threat from other companies, such as Amway, who were also granted direct-selling licenses in 2007, seem less compelling. In 2008, an internal whistle-blower made

charges about improper payments by the local Avon China office to
the Chinese government, including payments to Chinese officials for
arranging meetings with Andrea. Andrea disclosed, "We are volun-
tarily conducting an internal investigation that commenced in June
2008. The allegation is that certain travel, entertainment and other expenses may have been improperly involved in connection with China
operations."[2] Avon retained outside counsel under the oversight of
the Audit Committee of the board to conduct the investigation. It
extended through 2011, when it was expanded to other countries,
including Brazil, Mexico, Argentina, India, and Japan. The US Securities and Exchange Commission (SEC) opened its own investigation under the Foreign Corrupt Practices Act (FCPA), and that's when
things went from bad to worse.

Naturally, news of this investigation did not help Avon's stock price
or its image in China. The whole incident reads a bit like a bad TV
movie: around the same time in 2008, Chinese officials announced that
they had uncovered a major corruption ring of government officials
involved in licensing foreign companies in China. It is rumored that a
mistress of one of the officials was not happy that her lover refused to
marry her, so she blew the whistle on all the corrupt officials, some of
whom went to prison. The Chinese media then linked Avon's internal
investigation announcement with their country's corruption ring.

Though there's some debate about how much Avon executives
knew about the corruption and whether they practiced full or partial
disclosure, some industry observers have speculated that the real concern was a lack of business discipline and rigorous financial controls
and processes. Andrea had also refused throughout the years to intervene and reshape the China leadership team and moderate their overly
directive leadership style, even though others at Avon had urged her to
do so as far back as early 2000. In addition, a 2012 civil suit filed on
behalf of City of Brockton Retirement System, Metropolitan Water
Reclamation District Retirement Fund, and Louisiana Municipal Po-
lice Employees' Retirement System alleged that the company failed to

install the proper Foreign Corrupt Practices Act policies, controls, and training in what was known to be an at-risk market.

The board was concerned about the investigation but felt confident that Cramb was a strong CFO and that the appropriate internal controls had since been put in place. In fact, many senior Avon executives remained confident in the China strategy and policies. Sales were on an upswing, and the combination of Andrea's Chinese heritage and the seemingly strong Taiwanese team at the helm created the impression that things would work out.

Avon's local leaders weren't naïve. They knew that bribes were an accepted way of doing business in China and other parts of the world and had heard rumors that some of their competitors had bent the rules to obtain business favors. Speaking generally, businesspeople in China were often focused on pleasing their bosses above all else, and to that end, plenty of actions that would be frowned upon in the West raised nary an eyebrow. Given this awareness, Avon had implemented company-wide ethics training and other measures in 2004 to prevent its employees from violating any laws or moral standards.

The company as a whole, though, was focused on capitalizing on the direct-selling opportunity in China, and this focus turned into a kind of business myopia where tangential issues—such as how a company operated successfully in a foreign culture—were not addressed as well as they might have been. In China as well as other countries such as Brazil, Russia, Turkey, and the Philippines, Avon's business was growing. In this strong business environment, it was difficult for anyone to question the ethics of certain practices and be taken seriously.

TRANSFORMING TENSIONS

It was hard for Avon employees to imagine another financial free fall, given how fast the company was growing—7.5 percent in 2006 and 13.4 percent in 2007. Even when the 2008 recession hit, revenue growth was at 5.7 percent. Buoyed by these results, but knowing it was not enough, Andrea launched a $340 million ad campaign in 2007 titled "Hello Tomorrow," Avon's largest global ad campaign ever. It drove home her vision of brand, upgrading the company's image while also recruiting representatives. Celebrities such as tennis stars Venus and Serena Williams and actress Salma Hayek served as spokespersons, and Reese Witherspoon served as Avon's global ambassador.

Yet all this glitz and glamour couldn't mute the rumbling in the ranks—or in the executive offices. The new ad campaign exacerbated the tension between the old guard and new guard; the former group didn't like some of the new arrivals' big egos and their disrespect of the company's traditions and values. Much of the veteran staff felt diminished and undervalued when new people came in to fix the problems that existing staff had failed to solve. In addition, those with direct-selling expertise believed that the new processes, which may have been successful in consumer packaged goods companies, were not appropriate for a direct-selling company with a representative structure.

On top of this, these transformational moves strained representative loyalty. As the Avon brochure deemphasized gifts, toys, and home products in favor of beauty items and jewelry, representatives grimaced. These products were money-makers for them, and while the beauty emphasis might reshape the brand in positive ways, it seemed like this effort was taking money out of their pockets.

So many people were clamoring for Andrea's attention that it became a heated competition, and those who lost out sulked and shouted. Some felt she was playing favorites and politics. The executive team didn't engender trust, and some members didn't seem to trust each other. In fact, one of Andrea's direct reports was surreptitiously referred to as Lucifer by a number of both senior and middle managers. This was a far cry from the harmony and healthy debate that had existed earlier in her tenure. Country general managers, too, felt their roles had been diminished. Though they were still responsible for P&L, they believed they were now spending their time supporting corporate initiatives rather than being supported by headquarters. One longtime general manager said, "You used to be able to tell New York when they were wrong and be listened to. At that point [during the second half of Andrea's tenure], you were just told to agree or you were fired."

All transforming organizations experience some of these tensions and conflicts. Could Andrea have reduced them by doing things differently? Possibly. But when change of this scale is called for, a certain level of upset is inevitable. The larger question is whether Andrea was the right CEO to be orchestrating this transformation. Liz Smith was on board and ready to take over, but at least at this point in her career, she didn't possess Andrea's charisma, her international savvy, or her leadership maturity. With a recession looming, the board most likely urged Andrea to stay, preferring to stick with the known and still-revered CEO.

If Andrea had departed in 2008, she would have left with her reputation and halo fully intact. In fact, she would have left a hero. Yet, leaders aren't always aware of when to stay and when to go, and the board and consultants may not be able or willing to provide direction in this sensitive area.

LEADERSHIP LESSONS LEARNED

1. *Question regularly and objectively whether a leader is the right person at the right time.* CEOs that are successful early on often err on the side of staying too long rather than not long enough. They want to leave behind a legacy, they want to achieve their objectives, they want to enjoy the perks of the job. Yet in the volatile business environment of the twenty-first century, situations change quickly, and the person who was right for the job when he was hired may not be just a few years later. Boards and other advisors need to recognize this fact, even if a leader does not. Boards need to push

for multiple successors. In addition, they have to ask the tough questions, such as if a particular leader possesses the skills and vision to take the company where it needs to go in the next five years. Andrea certainly was the right person for the job when she was hired, and she turned the company around, and though she was more of a growth than a turnaround leader, she managed to use the "fire herself" advice to change and become the leader Avon needed in 2005. What isn't certain is whether she, Liz Smith, or an outsider would have been the best CEO in 2008 or 2009. It was asking a lot of Andrea to turn around the company again. She was so connected with representatives and staff that it was questionable whether she could make the tough decisions that would affect a significant percentage of employees negatively.

2. *Don't ignore the early warning signs, as painful as heeding those signs may be.* One of the biggest challenges for leaders is replacing an executive who generates strong short-term results but may become a long-term liability. This type of person is right in one way but wrong in another. Andrea was unwilling to address the leadership deficiencies of the China team with the speed and decisiveness that hindsight indicates was necessary. More than that, though, the China team had been chosen for their expertise in retail. When direct selling became the priority, it was apparent that they lacked expertise in that area. The head of China continued in his role, even though some tough questioning would have revealed he lacked deep direct-selling expertise and the leadership skills required to manage the China team during the transition from retail. The signs were there that, ultimately, his negatives outweighed his positives, especially as the company was changing. As difficult

as it may be to heed these signs, it is worse to rationalize or ignore them.

3. *Bring in the needed skills at the top, but not at the expense of senior leadership team cohesiveness.* Avon required an infusion of fresh skills, but a significant divide existed between the old and new guards. Veteran staff referred to the new executives Andrea brought in as the "Kraft mafia" (a number of them, like Liz Smith, came from Kraft), and the perception was that they knew little about the direct-selling model and didn't value it or the culture as much as the veterans. At least some of the new senior staffers thought of the veterans as stuck in the past with a narrow range of skills, and one of them remarked that it was common knowledge that the new regime's attitude was that if "you have been here more than ten years, you must not be that good or you would have left long ago." Consequently, the senior team did not operate synergistically. Leaders need to find ways to foster a collaborative environment, both by managing the relationships of their senior staff and by hiring people who are good collaborators. Andrea recognized the need to orchestrate the interplay of insiders and outsiders but at times struggled to create the right balance.

4. *Make sure there are dreamers and doers at the top. Too often in organizations, the CEO is a visionary who can't execute or an implementer who lacks vision. Leadership ambidexterity is crucial today.* When companies can't dream, they are ploddingly effective. When companies can't do, they are innovative to little purpose. From 1999 to 2004, Andrea was the dreamer and Susan, her COO, was the doer. It was the perfect match. Sometimes a CEO possesses both qualities, but more often, the CEO needs to find one or more people to complement her particular ability. Interestingly, Andrea the dreamer seemed to lose confidence or

enthusiasm for her vision during her middle years as CEO and didn't propose the types of bold plans and programs that marked her earlier years. The opportunities for big initiatives were there—India represented a huge direct-selling market but competitor Unilever was capitalizing on it to a much greater extent than Avon. If Andrea was gun-shy because of the failure of her retail initiative or because she had lost some of her willingness to take risks due to the downturn, then she should have brought another dreamer into the company.

5. *When embarking on transformational change, evolve the culture and not just the programs, policies, and processes.* In her first five years on the job, Andrea heeded this lesson. Just as she created a more integrated organization, she also began creating a more disciplined and fact-based culture. Most likely, however, she didn't move fast enough, and poor post-2005 results forced her to reemphasize centralized control. Part of the problem, too, was that it was never quite clear what Avon was transforming to. Did it aspire to be Unilever, or did it want to be the best direct seller? This identity crisis continued to plague the company throughout Andrea's reign. Without certainty about where the change was headed, it's difficult to evolve the culture on a parallel path. As one Avon employee noted, the organization was "half-pregnant and never fully came to term." Making cultural evolution even more difficult, Avon had been run historically as an entrepreneurial company and operated like a holding company. All sorts of behaviors were tolerated in this historical setting, including a senior leader's wife who operated her own business on an Avon site. As a culture that relied on relationships to get things done, too, formal processes had always taken a back seat, so it was difficult to impose strict financial controls and

oversight. Evolving this type of culture into one that was its opposite creates an even greater degree of difficulty. The real challenge, then, is preserving the spirit and norms that made a company great while changing other aspects of the culture so that it dovetails with where the company is headed when it reaches transformational maturity.

6. *Be able to fire yourself.* Ram Charan's advice and the title of this chapter is worth repeating and analyzing. In these stress-filled, chaotic times, leaders may be loath to do something different, to take a significant risk. They cleave to their tried-and-true approach, even when it's not working, or not working as well as it should. It is impossible to underestimate how difficult it must have been for Andrea to leave work one day and come back the next with a fresh leadership mindset. Downsizing, de-layering, and reducing costs weren't part of her leadership modus operandi. Andrea was all about the brand and migrating to the "masstige" market, which meant spending on advertising. She was also all about motivating and pleasing others, not reprimanding them or firing them. Yet she fired the old Andrea and came back with a version that was similar to the old one in some ways but much different in other aspects. Leaders who fire themselves must engage in serious reflection about who they are and who they must become. They must use that reflection as a catalyst for adjusting at least some significant leadership behaviors so they are more in tune with a changing organization.

SIX

THE FALL

2009–2012

GREAT LEADERS ARE RESILIENT, AND ANDREA EXEMPLIFIED THIS QUALITY AS THE RECES-sion took hold and Avon struggled on a number of fronts. Despite the clouds, Andrea seemed capable of leading yet another turnaround. At the beginning of this period, her halo still shone brightly, and many board members, senior managers, and employees in addition to ana-lysts and other outsider observers were still firmly in her corner.

Andrea's actions encouraged this faith. The prospect of turning around the company's fortunes yet again energized her, and she began mounting one of her trademark campaigns to generate support and lift morale. Andrea probably would have made a terrific political leader; she possessed a Clintonesque charisma and the strategic acumen of a top operative.

Yet even the most popular politicians can be defeated, and usu-ally for more than one reason. Andrea didn't suddenly become a bad leader. Instead, she was confronted by a series of negative events that overwhelmed her. In addition, she may not have had the senior team that she needed and she most likely fell prey to some bad advice from her advisors. Andrea may have been able to weather one or even two of these events, but their cumulative effect was too much to overcome. Huge legal fees from the Foreign Corrupt Practices Act (FCPA) investigation, an ill-advised acquisition, a failure to invest sufficiently in Avon's infrastructure, and other factors such as declining sales in key markets all conspired against Andrea's best efforts.

And Andrea did make an effort. She had planned to stay only ten years as CEO, and initially Liz Smith was the heir apparent. When Liz left to pursue CEO opportunities elsewhere in 2009 there were no other successors waiting in the wings so Andrea had little choice but to clean up the unfinished FCPA investigation and buckle down to drive growth and transformation in the midst of the recession.

RECRUITING AN ARMY OF AVON REPS

Andrea termed her strategy to recruit a larger number of new representatives during the economic downturn the "Recession Playbook." It was typical Andrea, brilliantly simple. The idea made perfect sense for Avon, because historically, the company had prospered when the economy went south. Not only were women eager to trade down from more expensive department store products to less expensive ones, but some wanted the extra income that being an Avon representative could provide. Despite concern about budgets during this time, Andrea took advantage of heavily discounted advertising rates (the automakers pulled their ads at the last minute) and ran an $800,000 Avon recruitment ad during the Super Bowl. With four out of every ten viewers being women over 18, many jobless, she knew that presenting the Avon opportunity in a compelling ad campaign would be a sure win. Rather than focus only on product ads or cut back advertising because of the recession, Andrea took a bold marketing stance, and it paid off. One million new representatives signed up, giving the company a total of nine million representatives worldwide.

Unfortunately, the new reps were never trained—at least not well enough to start selling at solid levels. Some critics wondered if this was the other side of Andrea's modus operandi—spectacular, bold programs with insufficient operational follow-up.

At the time, though, these criticisms were muted, mostly because Andrea was launching other bold initiatives simultaneously, such as Smart Value and Beauty on a Budget. These initiatives focused on creating specific Avon products that sold for less than $5, an approach designed to capitalize on the shrinking discretionary spending of customers in Avon's target market. In every corner of the company, new programs and policies were being launched.

Yet, at the end of 2009, the numbers were down, and other problems were surfacing. Revenue had declined 3 percent, and overall profit was down 24 percent. Though the critical overseas markets were doing okay, China revenue was up only 1 percent, as the retail and direct-selling operations took business away from each other. In addition, inconsistent pricing and confusing brand positioning hurt. In China's first-tier cities, Avon was seen as a middle-low end brand. In the more rural areas, Avon was facing increased competition from local players or multinationals such as Amway, who had more local, customized strategies in place. In Brazil, Avon was combating aggressive challenges by local direct seller Natura as well as Unilever. The data from 2010 show that Natura, the market leader, had a 14.4 share of the beauty market, with Unilever at 9.8 and Avon at 9.7 in a country where Avon had once been the market leader. Since 2004, Natura had been the market leader and outpaced Avon's growth in the market since 2007. On top of that, Liz Smith had left the company, and no one had replaced her as CEO-in-waiting. And the China bribery investigation hung over the company like a Damoclean sword; it was costing $7–$8 million a month.

Rumors of a takeover by L'Oreal surfaced in October 2010, and although they were never substantiated, it unsettled the environment. Andrea was looking hard for fresh ways to grow the company, and she decided the time was right to pursue the strategy she had long favored as a catalyst for growth: acquisitions.

THE ROAD TO $20 BILLION

Andrea had always favored acquisitions as a path for growth and even though she had brought people into Avon over the years who had specific mergers and acquisition (M&A) skills, including CFO Chuck Cramb, the time had never been right to use them (some observers have speculated that she got cold feet on the brink of some major deals). In 2010, though, the opportunities arose to acquire companies that could potentially move Avon into premium markets—a long sought-after goal. Andrea was fond of naming her programs and the "Road to $20 billion" was her label for the strategy designed to help the company double its revenues in five years via acquisitions and new growth strategies such as a separate global business focused on baby-related products.

Yet this road was littered with obstacles. For instance, Avon formed a new unit to launch the global baby business, but it was disbanded after two years due to lack of resources and uncertainty about the viability of the business. In addition, the company implemented a service model transformation initiative to provide better and faster product delivery to the representatives, as well as model a new way of doing business in the next ten years. But the representatives responded that they wanted the company to fix what was broken—the foundation—rather than come up with something new. The representatives wanted their orders in the box when they needed them. As one former senior leader said, "Zappos and Amazon can get women the products they order in 24 hours, and at Avon it was still taking 2–3 weeks." Despite this feedback, Andrea created a campaign around the service model transformation and other initiatives, encouraging people to embrace them through group talks and one-on-one conversations. Once again, she was trying to rally the troops, but this time the magic seemed to have worn thin. Employees were skeptical, recognizing the fundamental problems in the business that needed to be fixed. One former senior leader remarked, "We seemed to be always enamored with the new versus fixing what's broken." Another said, "The company had too many dreamers and not enough doers." Many of the initiatives eventually lost their funding.

In 2010, Avon made three acquisitions. The largest was Silpada, a home party sales, upmarket silver jewelry company that was profitable with high margins. Avon bought Silpada for $650 million and was criticized in some quarters for overpaying as well as for planning on running it as a separate versus an integrated business. Avon had always done well with jewelry globally and the margins were good, but within a year of the purchase, silver prices shot up from $15/$16 an ounce to $45/$46 an ounce. So not only was the cost too high for many Avon customers, but neither Silpada's designs nor its higher price points caught on with the base. Avon took a $263 million write-down in 2011.

The two other acquisitions were UK-based high-end skin care product company Liz Earle and Tanya Tilia, a small baby and mom product startup. While they may have made sense from branding perspectives, they represented significant drains on the company finances, and Avon ended up having to borrow money to pay dividends in 2011, creating accumulated debt issues the following year.

Initially there were no horrendous mistakes to point to. The first half of 2010 was solid, and the jury was still out on these acquisitions. But there were cracks in the foundation. Given Avon's global reach, they always had one market where something went wrong—a down economy, currency devaluations, a political upheaval, a restriction on direct selling. But in 2010, these problems began cropping up in multiple overseas markets.

Brazil and Russia, Avon's two top markets, were experiencing declining sales. Brazil was struggling because of service disruptions due largely to technology issues (implementation of an enterprise planning system and a government-mandated e-invoicing system). While all direct sellers in Brazil were experiencing problems because of the new government system, Avon was suffering more than the others, largely because of its outdated technology. As a former Avon Brazil leader stated, "The systems were held together with band-aids." The former leader went on to say that the local team had a few years to prepare for the implementation of the e-invoice system but started only six months before the government-mandated rollout. It seemed the local team had underestimated the task and the impact of the legacy systems. Andrea admitted in an investor call that Brazil's rapid growth as a market had outpaced the investment in the infrastructure; the toll on the outdated systems had taken her and others by surprise. But there were other issues as well. IT talent and expertise were lost in the de-layering of a few years earlier, leading to poor project planning and implementation. The result was a sales decline of almost 8 percent.

During investor calls, analysts began to ask more pointed questions. Though they weren't combative or accusatory, they were no longer willing to give Andrea the benefit of the doubt. In fact, some of her tactics no longer worked. The analysts wanted to know why the company was unaware of what was taking place in Brazil until it was too late and losses were mounting. Avon's CFO generally responded with optimistic reports about the future, suggesting that another turnaround was imminent, but his remarks were greeted with doubt and skepticism.

Something was wrong, and the fact that the board met 11 times during 2010 versus its normal 4–5 times, suggested that it wasn't just the analysts who thought so.

TAKING RESPONSIBILITY VERSUS SCAPEGOATING

Even the best leaders engage in subtle forms of denial when facing crises. This is less possible when a crisis is public and events force leaders to make immediate decisions. But most major organizational problems simmer in the background. In these instances, leaders can ignore the problems by delegating responsibility to others or rationalize that the problems are minor and hope that they'll go away. Some leaders are fortunate in that these problems provide loud and clear early warning signs, giving them time to act before they become major issues. In other instances, though, the early warning signs are muted and easy to deny. Such was the case with Avon's China situation.

At the time, it seemed as if the damage could be contained. But in 2010, it became evident to Andrea, the board, and others that they had a major problem on their hands and had to take action. It was publicly announced that four key members of the China team were put on administrative leave as a result of the FCPA investigation, including General Manager SK Kao, and all four were fired the next year.

In 2011, the SEC announced that they were opening up two separate investigations involving Avon. One focused on Avon's alleged bribing of Chinese government officials, a violation of the FCPA. The other revolved around information that Avon (i.e., CFO Chuck Cramb) allegedly shared with a financial analyst regarding the possible violation of Regulation Fair Disclosure Rules (this investigation was subsequently dropped by the SEC). In addition to Avon's internal investigation of FCPA violations, two other issues had emerged. The *Wall Street Journal* reported that an earlier memo had circulated among Avon executives—and Andrea was copied on it—that recommended increased company resources to match spending by competitors on travel and gifts for Chinese officials. Just as concerning, the court papers filed in the 2012 shareholder suit alleged that an Avon Latin America finance staffer threatened to blow the whistle on the company because of bribery allegations if the company didn't give him a better severance package.

Not only was a pattern of possible rules violations being established, but the shareholder suit also alleges that Avon covered up a draft audit report in the 2005–2006 time period which surfaced possible improper payments to the Chinese government. This alleged cover-up also posed a potential criminal offense and a grand jury was convened in February of 2012, although to date no criminal charges have been filed. By 2012, Avon had paid lawyers more than $250 million. As of mid-2013, that figure is close to $340 million. Cramb was fired, as was the head of global audit. Beyond the financial and personnel losses, the alleged improprieties in China continue to cast a pall over the company.

Perhaps the most disturbing aspect of the China situation was the departure of Ben Gallina. Certain senior executives exist in every organization who are respected by all for their talent and their personal integrity, and Ben was one of them at Avon.

Ben Gallina had started with the company in 1977 and worked his way up through the finance organization to eventually become senior VP for Western Europe, Middle East, Africa, Asia Pacific, and China. Ben was known as one of the strongest, most level-headed, and loyal of all of Andrea's senior team. He was able to sort through the complexity of the global, regional, and local debate to focus on what was most important. Andrea trusted and relied on him, especially to keep the China operations and SK Kao under control. Ben was a dedicated employee, committed to both the company and Andrea's vision for it. At his wedding, he said he loved three things: the woman he was now marrying, his late first wife, and Avon. Andrea liked and respected Ben, and she had attended his wedding. He had taken on every role asked of him and sacrificed both personally and professionally for the company.

In *The Maltese Falcon,* Humphrey Bogart's Sam Spade says, someone has to take the blame, to be the fall guy. In the case of Avon, that someone was Ben Gallina. The board mandated Andrea to act—he was put on administrative leave and then transitioned into retirement. That Ben would have done anything improper was inconceivable to those who knew him well. In fact, Ben once confided to me that his greatest fear in taking the Asia regional role was the fallout that might occur when he signed a company or government-issued document written in Chinese because he was unable to read what he was signing.

No doubt, the board was doing what it could to appease the SEC. Again, in hindsight, the board should probably have been more aggressive in trying to settle with the SEC and challenging outside counsel, rather than looking for someone to take the fall. Those close to the situation said that Andrea was instructed by her internal general counsel not to get overly involved in the investigation for her own protection. It's possible, however, that she could have used her star power and powers of persuasion to negotiate a deal. Instead, under the new CEO, Sheri McCoy, the SEC rejected Avon's $12 million offer to settle in 2013, and it will probably take a considerably larger sum of money to settle the case once and for all.

Part of the problem may have been that the legal process was leading the business rather than vice versa. Organizations tend to defer to their heavyweight law firms—this is especially true when they're facing a potential crisis—and fail to manage the process effectively. It's not that the lawyers were doing anything unethical. They were trying to help their client to the best of their ability. But when dealing with aggressive government agencies that are going after a corporation, the legal costs can be exorbitant and take money away from necessary business investments. The most effective course of action may be to settle early even if the company wants to fight the charges. It may mean instructing the attorneys to negotiate rather than defend. It may mean biting the bullet and doing whatever is necessary to appease a given governmental agency. Instead, Avon and the board let the process drag on for years, and it became a financial burden as well as a major distraction.

SHAKING THINGS UP

Even as the China scandal unfolded and then expanded to other markets, Andrea was focusing on other equally serious problems. In early 2011, she began making changes once again. Her presentation at the Consumer Analyst Greater New York conference provided her with a forum to announce an organizational restructuring that essentially put the direct-selling experts in the organization back in their old positions of power. In a sense, this was Andrea's acknowledgment that the pendulum had swung too far in the direction of brand and consumer packaged goods. She also appointed new general managers in both the United States and Russia, two of the three key markets in her plan to revitalize the company. She also introduced a new line, Avon Care, designed exclusively for emerging markets with both a price point and product portfolio (e.g. smaller sizes) focused on that segment's set of needs. For the struggling US market, Andrea implemented "one simple sales model," a multilevel approach designed to boost representative earnings. Direct-selling companies Herbal Life and Amway were growing at double-digit rates, and Avon was underperforming. Though none of these moves were made in a panic, they represented Andrea's decision to circle back to the old Avon. It wasn't that she actually wanted to return the company to the way it was when she joined, but she recognized that there was grumbling in the ranks of representatives and analysts. It had not been a good half year, and to her credit, Andrea reversed direction and responded to criticism. For instance, one common complaint was that the company had prioritized global over local, and to correct this imbalance, Andrea announced that responsibility for resource planning was being taken away from corporate and pushed down to the local markets.

Andrea also offered acknowledgment of fault in an effort to repair relationships internally. Andrea admitted that the company had not done a good job in Brazil. In that country, representatives often worked for other companies simultaneously, and they tended to favor the lead horse in their selling. She also admitted that the transition from nonbeauty to beauty products had been difficult and the strategy had failed to respond adequately to representative and customer needs in the midst of this change.

While things weren't great in the first two quarters, external criticism was muted. This changed in the third quarter after the announcement of the SEC's two investigations. The stock dropped 18 percent, and a highly combative analyst call the next day was a taste of things to come. In it, Citigroup analyst Wendy Nicholson made a remark that would follow Andrea around for months: "It strikes me that you guys are totally screwed up in so many ways, the change had to be radical."[1] In the coming days, other probing questions were asked: Why had Andrea not filled the vacant COO slot? Why should investors believe that the management and the board has any control over the business? Why, after ten years, didn't Andrea possess more insight into and control over the business? Why did all of this seem to be a surprise to so many?

Andrea's response was fair and accurate by finally recognizing that the system was patchwork and that IT systems had not kept pace with a more global, centralized organization structure. Most staff agreed that the lack of systems had hindered the pace of codifying many of the transformed processes. This also may have been a signal that she had swung the centralization pendulum too far without the talent and the infrastructure to execute it.

Andrea had ceased to be the keeper of the brand. Her focus had widened and deepened to include cash, inventory, management, and margins as the stock dropped 20 percent by 2011.

I BELIEVE, BUT DOES ANYONE ELSE?

Andrea still believed in making a splash. She'd always been masterful at creating events and dominating them, using them to motivate and excite. Still, in 2011 when she embarked on a worldwide "I Believe" tour to mark the company's one hundred twenty-fifth anniversary, some people at Avon scratched their heads. Given the investigations and business difficulties, they questioned whether the tour was money—or time—well spent by their beleaguered leader.

As one concerned employee remarked, "So what was that all about?"

Another Avon executive said he was asked to provide feedback about whether the company should fund a proposed $10–20 million Avon Voices online singing competition as part of the "I Believe" tour. He suggested that now might not be the best time, given the difficult financial challenges the company was facing. His input was ignored and wasn't sought again.

Avon managers from around the world were flown in to attend the finals of the Voices competition, and as usual, it was a terrific,

emotionally involving event that helped reaffirm people's commitment to Avon and what it stood for. Andrea was in fine form, but
one manager noticed that her face seemed troubled. Behind the smile
lurked a frown—perhaps she was thinking about the enormous cost
of the event, the lawyer's fees that were draining the company cof-
fers, and the analyst call the next day where she would have to deliver
more bad news.

After this event, Andrea took a step back. She seemed to detach
herself from the daily grind of running the business, scaling down her
enthusiasm and involvement. The tremendous pressure she was under
appears to have triggered her aloof derailer. Instead of providing ongoing communication to staff about the status of the business, Andrea
became less communicative and involved according to a number of
observers. The SEC investigation cast a long shadow. Analysts began
to call for a change at the top. A former sales executive recalled a presentation to Andrea and the senior team around this time where he
noticed that one of the team was paying more attention to his iPad
then to what he was saying. Andrea was attentive, but she was no longer
commanding the stage.

Yet she wasn't ready to leave quite yet, and no one was willing to
show her the door. Andrea may well have believed she had another
turnaround in her. She never lacked for confidence or optimism, and
so perhaps some part of her was still trying to formulate a new and
improved vision for the company. Even when things were at their
worst, Andrea continued strategizing, though not with the same focus
as before.

It's fair to ask why Avon's board didn't act. Part of the reason was
that Andrea was adept at handling her board, able to anticipate their
concerns and stay ahead of them. Although new board members had
been brought in, many had been in place for years, and Andrea had
developed close relationships with some. But even without them, she
would have been difficult to remove. For 12 years, she had personi-
fied Avon, saving the company twice and helping it double in size. In

addition, the board may have felt that Andrea had to stay in place until the SEC investigation was concluded.

Perhaps most significantly, no one else was ready to take over. The bench strength wasn't great; there was no obvious successor. Conducting a search would be expensive and time-consuming, and external CEOs are always a gamble, especially with an SEC investigation ongoing. Besides, a search would create uncertainty at a time when the board desperately wanted to create stability. They were eager to assuage disgruntled representatives, and many board members were still intensely loyal to, and a bit in awe of Andrea.

Still, the pressure to do something was intense, and after much discussion and debate Andrea and the board agreed on a transition plan. In December 2011, Andrea stepped down as CEO but retained her chairman title and significant responsibilities. For the next two years, her main focus would be high-level strategy and assisting with the new CEO transition. In essence, this allowed the board to have their cake and eat it too—a new CEO would be found and trained, but in the interim, Avon would benefit from having Andrea at the helm. By all accounts, Andrea handled her impending departure with grace and maturity.

Andrea must have recognized that this was the right thing to do, as evidenced by her statement when this announcement was made: "I believe the time is right to separate the chairman and CEO roles. . . . A new CEO will provide a fresh lens and additional operational and executive leadership."[2] Andrea never issued a public statement like this lightly. It was a well-considered acknowledgment that, just as she had provided a fresh perspective when she had been named Avon's CEO, the company needed someone else to provide that now. She was aware that she had lost some control and that making this move was best for her and for the organization.

The reaction was mixed. The stock price jumped 5 percent immediately afterward, suggesting that investors thought Andrea's giving up the CEO job was good for the company. Former CEO and

Andrea mentor Jim Preston had sent a letter to the board that leaked
and proved embarrassing. It said in part, "How could you go through
five or six years of the performance that they've had and not begin to
ask serious questions, and say our hires are not right and our operating
systems are not right?"[3] Another former Avon CEO, David Mitchell,
chimed in with his belief that "the split CEO-Chairman structure (was)
a stupid arrangement" and that it would make the board's search for a
successor nearly impossible.[4] Some Avon employees, too, were angry at
Andrea for financial reasons. One employee said, "I was so loyal [to]
and confident in the company that I put a large majority of my 401k in
stock, and now I've seen the value of my retirement savings dwindle."

At the same time, other employees—especially senior staff who
worked closely with her—remained fiercely loyal and blamed the
downward spiral on bad advisors or external circumstances beyond
anyone's control. Perhaps just as important, Andrea was a great leader
in the eyes of many business journalists, consultants, analysts, and
other CEOs; she was especially admired and emulated by other female
executives. Some, however, were eager to toss her aside.

The year ended on a confused note. While revenues managed to
move upward by 4 percent, operating profit declined by 20 percent.
Perhaps the biggest change, though, and one that suggested a leader
with a different set of skills and experiences should be in charge, was
that 83 percent of Avon's revenues in 2011 came from outside of the
United States, almost 70 percent of that from developing countries.
This contrasts with the 60 percent US and 40 percent foreign markets revenues that characterized Andrea's first year as CEO. It's worth
noting that China, once projected to be a market that would serve as
Avon's growth engine, was down 20 percent. In 2007, Avon in China
had a beauty market share of 6.5 percent, and in 2011 it had dropped
to 1.9 percent. In 2011 Amway had sales in China of $4.2 billion com-
pared to Avon's sales of $300 million. At one time the Avon ladies in
China were famous and university students aspired to sell Avon. By
2011, Avon China's image was tarnished, employees were not proud to

work there, and the company had abandoned direct selling and gone back to retail and may just do online sales going forward.

At the start of Andrea's tenure, the ad slogan had insisted that the company was "not your mother's Avon." Increasingly, it seemed, it was also no longer Andrea's.

AN AWKWARD EXIT

Before Andrea departed, Kimberly Ross, formerly CFO at Royal Ahold was hired as CFO, replacing Chuck Cramb who was fired because of the bribery probe. She did a good job of getting the financials in order, and the business seemed to be stabilizing in early 2012. In fact, Avon's low share price and other factors encouraged takeover attempts, the most serious by competitor Coty, who at one time was rumored to have been in negotiations for a merger with Avon and then who turned the tables and became the aggressor. They made a good offer and then upped it, but the Avon Board rejected both. Given that Coty's best offer was a 20 percent premium above the current stock price, their rejection was perplexing. Coty eventually withdrew their offer, and the company continued on its independent path.

There was much speculation about who was blocking the takeover. Some observers blamed Andrea, though it's difficult to understand what her motivation might have been. Some blamed the board, suggesting that Coty and others would have been privy to Avon's books in a takeover, and the board didn't want to disclose what was there, especially information related to the SEC investigation. Others claim that there was in-fighting among board member factions and that lead director Fred Hassan's departure the following year was due in part to this internal dispute.

Whatever the reason, Avon continued on with Andrea fading into the background while Kimberly took on a more prominent role, assuming some COO duties in addition to her CFO role. Though Kimberly hadn't been on the job long, she possessed the financial insight and outsider perspective to view Avon in a fresh light. When she looked at the organization, she said she saw a hybrid—a company that was a unique blend of consumer packaged goods and direct selling. Finding the sweet spot in the middle of these two business types struck her as the best strategic approach, and her initial strategic suggestions implied that Avon had moved too far in the global packaged goods direction.

The board finally named a new CEO, Sheri McCoy, formerly worldwide chairman of the pharmaceuticals group of Johnson & Johnson. The company's stock went up by 7 percent when her appointment was announced in April 2012. Certainly most new CEOs would not welcome outside interference and it was more than a bit symbolic that Andrea moved her office, far away from Sheri, tucked away in a corner. The next six months were awkward, in that people still called Andrea for decisions even though she no longer had that power. Though Andrea and Sheri treated each other with respect, it was an unhealthy situation. Andrea seemed to want to be helpful and tried to stay out of the way to make the transition as smooth as possible, but there was little she could do. In October, 2012, six months after Sheri's appointment as CEO, Andrea stepped down as chairman.

Sheri's experience at Johnson & Johnson was useful, in that they were a more decentralized company than Avon as well as a more contemporary one. By that I mean that Johnson & Johnson employed more modern strategies in a variety of areas, that is, they favored testing and learning over big global rollouts and balancing global scale with local customization. Based on her training as well as her first-hand observations in Avon markets throughout the world, Sheri shifted the company's direction. She recognized that, at least to a certain extent, management had lost sight of what both customers and representatives required. Sheri was willing to tailor products and methods to markets—in Latin America, she approved greater emphasis on fragrances—in response to local preferences. Sheri was also willing to jettison things that weren't working; she exited poor-performing markets such as Ireland and Vietnam, and sold Silpada, the relatively recent jewelry acquisition, back to the cofounders for $85 million (Avon had paid $650 million for it only a few years earlier). Getting rid of expensive global celebrities, making significant investments in IT and social media, and other tactics were all part of a clear break with the previous administration. How all these moves will turn out for Sheri and Avon is impossible to know at this writing, but they do seem more suited to the environment in which the company is operating.

GREATNESS IN PERSPECTIVE

In a sense, Andrea was like a great professional sports coach who has a run of championships and then sees her team falter and fail. Perhaps her players aged, were injured, or simply couldn't perform as well, or they traded away a star for financial reasons, or the general manager drafted poorly. Or perhaps the coach failed to motivate as well as she once did or continued to run a system that no longer suited the players she had. Whatever the cause, a great coach, like a great CEO, doesn't just lose it one day. Instead, circumstances change, and greatness doesn't protect anyone from failure.

Was Andrea responsible for her own demise? It's difficult to say. Some executives who worked for her were furious because they held her responsible for losing their jobs or the declining value of their 401(k) plans. Others remained stalwart supporters, believing that her double turnaround success, charisma, and marketing genius made her a candidate for the CEO hall of fame. There's no question that Andrea was a pioneering female CEO who paved the way for other women leaders. There's also no question that she made mistakes. She was a visionary leader, yet it appeared she couldn't see that the company lacked essential operations expertise and discipline once Susan Kropf, her COO, left and was not replaced.

So what went wrong? Why did a great leader fail? The following seven factors come to mind:

1. The China FCPA investigation that then broadened into other countries—the financial cost, the impact on the company's image in China, and the shadow it cast over the entire organization.

2. The IT debacle in Brazil—emblematic of the company's failure to invest properly in infrastructure. Even more significant, perhaps, was that some fundamentals were being overlooked or given short shrift.

3. The cash drain—paying too much to acquire Silpada was one of the most costly mistakes.

4. Lack of a successor—the board, Andrea, and the head of Human Resources bears this responsibility.

5. Talent drain—first a result of delayering and then a result of alienating direct-selling experts.

6. The dimming of the halo—because of all the problems Avon experienced and the cultural erosion, Andrea could no longer rally the troops as she had in the past. The representatives were no longer in Andrea's thrall—or at least they weren't as unquestioningly loyal as they had been.

7. Failing to execute and acknowledging the failure to execute. After Susan Kropf's departure, the company struggled to implement its strategies. Andrea's vision and ideas were still powerful, but putting them into practice become more difficult than it had been.

I enumerate these factors not to assess blame—after all, every halo dims with enough time—but to facilitate thinking about the larger leadership issues that Andrea faced. Every company has to confront the challenges of a CEO search, potential scandals, evolving technology, and so on. More to the point, the cumulative impact of these factors can swamp even the best companies and leaders unless they're aware and prepared to deal with them.

As we move into the next section of the book and examine these issues more closely, the following questions and answers offer my analytical perspective about Andrea's rise and fall as a leader.

Q: What were Andrea's overall strengths as a leader?

A: First and foremost, Andrea was inspirational and charismatic. She truly believed in Avon's vision of women and their financial independence and made that a primary focus for the organization. Employees worldwide rallied around Andrea's articulation of this higher purpose. As a visionary, she was adept at painting a picture of what could be, and as a trusting, caring leader, she was able to align individuals so they could overcome obstacles. Finally, she was inclusive and humble—the former made people feel empowered, the latter made them loyal and supportive.

Q: What were Andrea's weaknesses?

A: Like many leaders, Andrea's strengths were at times overleveraged and turned into weaknesses. Her strategic capability was not always balanced with an ability to execute. Put another way, she was great at articulating the dream but not at developing the set of concrete actions to get there. She also was overly optimistic, which sometimes hurt her ability to see situations clearly. I've also alluded to Andrea's Aloof and Pleaser derailers—in good times, they could be strengths, in stressful times they prevented her from making the tough calls on the culture as well as on people. When Andrea blinked—that is, when she couldn't make hard choices that would potentially alienate people—her Pleaser derailer was the problem.

Q: Did Andrea stay too long?

A: Yes. Although the research is mixed on the optimal CEO tenure (Disney's CEO just got a contract extension for a total of 11 years as CEO, while Steve Ballmer of Microsoft left after 13 years), most seem to believe it is somewhere between 9 and 10 years. Though Andrea reinvented herself successfully and prolonged her effectiveness, this trick can only work once or twice. Eventually, longevity breeds comfort, routines, and nearsightedness. Andrea's skills and experiences did not prepare her for the new beauty market, where more individuals are purchasing products over the Internet and through mobile apps, social media has become a channel in and of itself, big box retailers continue to dominate, and direct selling is a viable channel for some but not all markets.

Q: Why didn't Andrea reshape her team when it became evident they weren't producing results?

A: Andrea trusted the senior staff she brought in during 2005 and perhaps felt that it was better to have individuals that knew the business working on solving the problems than to bring in new people who would have a steep learning curve. It's also possible that she was overly optimistic about her team's abilities. Perhaps her biggest mistake from a talent standpoint was failing to replace Susan Kropf or Susan's skill set when she retired. Although she was only one person, the loss of Susan and her skill set turned out to be devastating. At the time, though, Andrea may not have fully grasped how critical Susan's role was or the synergistic power of their relationship. Her knowledge of all aspects of the business and the P&L levers was never replaced. Avon had become dependent on one individual for execution, and no company should place all their chips on a single employee, no matter how skilled that employee is. Bench strength is crucial, especially during volatile times.

Q: Why didn't the board do more?

A: For many years, the company was experiencing double-digit growth. This made for a supportive and confident board. When things started to go wrong, they seemed to drift into denial and then became overly cautious. In addition, although the board had several long-tenured directors, it lacked directors with deep direct-selling expertise. They may have also lacked the right metrics to track business and financial performance. Many trends and events seemed to come as a surprise to both Andrea and the board, which suggests that there also were not enough early warning signs that triggered appropriate responses from leadership.

The answers to these questions suggest that when it comes to leadership, greatness guarantees nothing, at least not in the long run. Even the best leaders have flaws, and they need to be aware of these flaws and try to manage the negative behaviors they produce. The longer your run as CEO, the more likely it is that these flaws will do damage. I'm not absolving Andrea of her mistakes, merely pointing out that not many CEOs can survive for 13 years these days unless they have strong support of their boards (which Andrea had until the last year or two), keen awareness of their personal derailers, and a certain amount of luck.

In her departing email to Avon employees, Andrea wrote, "My love affair with Avon will never end."[5] I have no doubt that was a sincere sentiment and one that kept her at the company a little longer than was good for both her and the organization.

LEADERSHIP LESSONS LEARNED

1. *Find a way to have at least two CEO successors in the pipeline trained and ready to go.* This is tricky, but it's necessary in today's volatile environment. Too often, the ideal candidate is groomed internally or hired from the outside but something gums up the works—the CEO decides not to retire or the successor takes a CEO position at another organization. To their credit, the Avon Board was heavily involved in talent planning and regularly discussed succession planning issues.

They were the ones who insisted on hiring a high profile executive (Liz Smith) who could be groomed to take over from Andrea. Unfortunately, when Liz Smith departed it left the pipeline dry. Ideally, the CEO, Human Resources, and the board will take responsibility for having more than one candidate on board and trained to take over. Large companies such as GE or Johnson & Johnson often use the horse race model, setting up competitions between a number of executives to determine who should be the next CEO. This way, even the runner-up is often well-qualified for the CEO position. Whatever the tactic, the key is not to just identify candidates but to give them the experiences required and the necessary coaching to prepare them for the job. This requires planning.

2. *Lead with an optimistic heart but a realistic head.* Andrea's positive attitude and confidence in herself and the company galvanized others to follow. Most people work better and harder for optimistic leaders than pessimistic ones (or those who are neutral, for that matter). But optimism needs to be tempered with realism. It took Avon too long to get out of markets such as Japan because, despite the data, management was sure that they could "fix" things. In China, too, the constant, optimistic refrain was that though the market was complex, it was also huge, and Avon had the brand and resources to capitalize on it. This optimism prevented leadership from looking at the market realistically—at seeing how the Avon model may not have been well-suited to the culture and the business practices there. Moving from a retail model back to direct-selling may have been too difficult a change. The key here is that leaders must ask the tough questions and question their own assumptions: Am I doing something wrong as

a leader? Do we need expertise we lack? Is there something about our processes or policies that has become an obstacle? Do we have what it takes as an organization to capitalize on this opportunity?

3. *Remember that big is not necessarily better.* Big leaders want to do big things. "Make no small plans; they have little magic to stir men's blood. . . . ," said Daniel Burnham, Chicago's famous architect and urban planner in the early part of the twentieth century. Andrea was great at stirring people's blood with her big, bold initiatives. Yet in her later years with the company, it may not have been wise to spend the money that her programs required. The Avon Voices competition, for instance, cost a purported $10–20 million at a time the organization desperately needed funds to upgrade their IT function. While the Voices competition fostered involvement and positive publicity, it probably could have been done on a much smaller scale at a much lower cost. Leaders need to recognize, and at time resist, their tendency to make a huge splash. Obviously, at times outsized programs are needed and provide motivation and buzz—Andrea proved the value of this approach in her first five years on the job. But there are also times when smaller is better, when a huge investment pays a less than optimal return. Toning it down on occasion allows leaders to save money; it also ensures that they'll avoid the monotony and eventual backlash that come with one big program after another.

4. *Find, value, and empower doers and detailers.* People like Andrea get all the attention, but people like COO Susan Kropf are just as valuable to organizations. It's not a coincidence that Andrea was at her best when Susan was at her side. Susan knew the business inside and out and had worked in almost

every part of the company. Because Andrea, like many visionary, charismatic leaders, didn't sweat the small stuff, she needed a detail-oriented doer like Susan. During the last few years of Andrea's tenure, Susan was gone, as were other detail-oriented executives. For this reason, operations and execution suffered. In addition, Avon was a relationship-based company, which is a strength in some ways, a weakness in others. It was the latter when bold targets and goals would be set, but no well-thought-out plan existed, and few managers were willing and able to drive people toward objectives. The culture of kindness and affiliation often prevented anyone from cracking the whip and pushing employees toward tight deadlines and ambitious goals. Again, the culture fostered lots of dreams but no execution plans.

5. *Search for and recalibrate balance points regularly.* During Andrea's years at Avon, the company was faced with a series of balancing acts: between global and local, direct selling and consumer packaged goods, beauty and knickknacks, single-level and multilevel sales models, and building the brand and making money. Andrea did a good job of adjusting this balance early on, recognizing that it was going too far in the direction of direct selling, local markets, and so on. Sometimes, however, Andrea would push in one direction—such as retail—and the balance would get out of whack. Like many leaders, she had a vision she wanted realized—Avon as a beauty company focused on brands—and that desire tilted the balance. In the last few years, the company swung back and forth between two opposing poles without much planning or analysis—it was responding to events and situations. The best leaders maintain a high balance consciousness and adjust it proactively. They are acutely aware that they must

shift more toward global at one point, more toward local customization at another. Developing this agility isn't always easy, as leaders generally are biased in one direction or another, but in an uncertain, unpredictable environment, it's a crucial leadership skill.

PART TWO

BROADER LEADERSHIP LESSONS

NOW THAT YOU KNOW ALL ABOUT ANDREA JUNG'S RISE AND FALL AT AVON, CONSIDER THE story from a pure leadership perspective. Few CEOs face the number of challenges that Andrea did or find ways to meet those challenges successfully. Few CEOs are as charismatic and as savvy about using that charisma to achieve business goals. Few CEOs can help a company almost double in size during their tenure. And few CEOs fail as suddenly and publicly as Andrea did.

So there's a lot to analyze, and in the first section, I extrapolated leadership lessons that corresponded to each phase of Andrea's tenure at Avon. Now, I'd like to take that analysis one step further. Andrea's story raises issues that don't fit neatly into the chronology but transcend it—issues such as CEO selection and succession, executive team challenges, organizational culture, women in leadership roles, and the global challenges in the twenty-first century. I spoke to a wide range of other leaders about these issues to help connect Andrea's experiences to the ones your organization is likely to experience.

If the first section could be described as "What Andrea did," then this second section could be described as "What you would do if you were in Andrea's position." For example, if your organization's strategy has changed, is the CEO who was hired five years ago still the best CEO for the job? How are you handling some of the common paradoxes that exist in your organization? Are your long-standing traditions and organizational culture helping you reach your goals or interfering with them? What can you do to avoid some of the traps that Andrea fell into?

I've also included some take-home elements to help you apply these lessons to your own organization. I hope the Beauty Queen's legacy will yield fresh insights into whatever leadership challenges you face.

SEVEN

RIGHT LEADERS, RIGHT TIME

ANDREA WAS INDISPUTABLY THE RIGHT LEADER FOR AVON BETWEEN 1999 AND 2005. Rarely has a CEO been so well matched to an organization. Andrea had exactly the right skills and traits to lead the company during these years, and the organization had just the right DNA to complement Andrea's strengths. Conversely, Andrea was the wrong leader for the company toward the end of her reign—her abilities didn't match up with many organizational needs, and her colleagues didn't fill in the gaps.

How can companies find their perfect leaders? And how can they make sure that this perfect leader remains well-suited to the top job as strategies, competitors, and other factors change?

I'm going to explore answers to both questions, but perhaps not in the way you expect. Finding a candidate to match the job specs has been the holy grail of CEO searches for decades. This is obviously important, but I'd suggest that other equally important tasks are often overlooked. Figuring out a given leader's "tilt" and how that dovetails with the organization's requirements is an assessment worth making in addition to the specs; helping develop a leader's "nontilt"—the areas where she's either weak or lacks interest—and making sure team members aren't attitudinal or talent clones of the leader is another. Ensuring organizations have the right leaders at the right time requires consciousness and diligence. It also requires a deliberate model to match leaders to the company's stage of growth.

A FLEXIBLE FRAMEWORK FOR LEADERSHIP AT THE RIGHT TIME

In my consulting work and teaching, I've found the following diagnostic tool especially useful in helping companies identify the individuals who are best suited to lead them. It follows the five growth stages most organizations experience:

1. Creativity—The initial stage of growth that usually occurs in the early days of a business. This period is characterized by informality and innovation. After a while, though, things start falling through the cracks, and a more formal structure becomes necessary. It's at this point that a manager is brought in who can install growth-facilitating formal processes and structure.

2. Direction—Organizational charts emerge, roles are clarified, and growth occurs. At some point, though, this growth often creates inefficiencies, slow decision making, and other negative fallout. As the organization's direction is identified and pursued, structure can become constraining, requiring leaders to redistribute power to lower levels in the organization and balance control with increased empowerment.

3. Delegation—If the previous stage was about structure, processes, and control, this one is about delegating responsibility closer to the market in a more decentralized way. Management moves the decision-making authority from corporate to more localized control, with the belief that those closest to the action are best able to make informed choices. This phase ends when scope and complexity make resource requirements unsustainable. As organizations delegate, they lose some control and need to balance decision making at the source closest to the customer, retain control, and not become too centrist.

4. Coordination—To manage growth during this phase, organizations often adopt a matrix or alternative structure instead of returning to stage 2, direction. This helps deal with scope and complexity but can also lead to bureaucratic inefficiencies and conflict over who is responsible for decisions. Here leaders must acknowledge and manage the natural tensions that exist between line and staff, global and local, and they must develop processes to cut through the bureaucracy and ensure speedy and efficient decision making.

5. Collaboration—The focus here is on getting closer to the customer, simplifying processes, and working collaboratively through informal teaming across the organization to solve problems. Leaders need to be nimble and establish early warning systems to indicate when the pendulum has swung too far toward overly local or global processes. Changing organization structure may be an effective response, or leaders may need to develop flexible teams and processes to respond to changing customer demands.[1]

When Charlie Perrin was CEO of Avon and when Andrea took over, the company was in Stage 3, or delegation. It was caught between the paradox of global and local, the global need to leverage economies of scale versus the need to meet local customer requirements. Most observers felt that Charlie chose global over local, placing an increasing amount of control in corporate hands. While this does achieve some key objectives—standardization, cost savings, and so on—it can alienate local managers who fear a "one size fits all" mandate.

At this growth stage, Avon needed a CEO who could walk the fine line between corporate and local. Andrea was a good fit for this stage in that she recognized the value of both corporate and local concerns and attempted to address both. You wouldn't know it from her resume or on an evaluation form, but she had an uncanny ability to walk fine lines and simultaneously think in terms of global, regional, and local. On

the one hand, she worked at developing higher-quality and more technologically sophisticated global products than the local markets could
produce. On the other hand, she valued working with local managers
and helping them meet the needs of their customers.

But the fourth growth phase—coordination—is complex. Avon
had attempted to work through a dense organization structure in the
2002–2004 time frame but by 2005 had ended up with too many management layers, high costs, and slower decision making. Avon then made
the mistake of course correcting by swinging to centralization as the
answer to reduce complexity and regain control. This resulted in a loss
of local market customer and representative focus and even slower decision making and bureaucratic processes. Andrea was no longer the right
leader at the right time. She was not especially adept at cutting through
red tape, a leadership requirement in this stage. When red tape becomes
too burdensome, country heads leave the company because they've lost
authority and feel they have become subservient to the bureaucracy. Decision making slows to a crawl, and customers leave for competitors. All
of this happened on Andrea's watch, and though she wasn't to blame
for a lot of it, she also wasn't the ideal leader for this growth phase.

What Avon needed was a CEO who could handle the operational
complexity that comes with coordination. It turned out that Sheri Mc-
Coy, Andrea's successor, has been this type of leader. She came from
Johnson & Johnson, a highly decentralized company. She also possesses
the competencies required for collaboration (phase 5) and has used
general headquarters staff more as consultants than order givers, transitioning the company to a more customer-centered structure, able to
meet local needs while leveraging economies of scale.

To facilitate selection and evaluation of leaders at each of these five
growth stages, take the following steps:

1. Identify the organization's growth stage and discuss the implications. Given the challenges of the stage, what specific skills are
   required? What types of changes—new policies, strategies, and

so on—does the leader need to implement to deal with the tensions emerging in the growing company?

2. Watch for warning signs of a disconnect between the leader and the company's growth stage. Slow decision making is a common warning sign, suggesting uncertainty about how to handle issues. A second warning sign is when people are confused about their roles and responsibilities. A third is when processes that once worked well are no longer effective (or as effective).

3. Determine if the solutions the leader is implementing fit with a given stage. For instance, a matrix structure is often a good solution in Stage 4 (coordination) but not a good approach in Stage 2 (direction).

CEO-COO: THE COMPLEXITIES OF A GREAT 1-2 PUNCH

Just as heroes often need a partner, some CEOs need COOs. No matter how brilliant or skilled the top executive in an organization might be, he or she is often missing something. Every Batman needs a Robin. Andrea's strengths as a marketer, brand builder, and charismatic visionary were complemented perfectly by COO Susan Kropf's operational expertise. Yet the pairing of these two leaders was more a happy accident than a carefully planned succession. In fact, then and now, boards often focus myopically on the CEO for a specific purpose or situation rather than finding the right mix of CEO and COO. Talent is also in short supply, so boards frequently don't have the luxury of having an immensely talented second in command who possesses the strengths that a CEO lacks.

Too often, boards and HR departments fail to keep the 1-2 combination in mind, both as a guiding selection principle and afterwards, as the organizational situation changes. As you may have noticed, the title of this chapter is plural—leaders rather than leader—and that's because it's the rare CEO who has the mix of expertise and experience to singlehandedly lead a company through a volatile environment. To find the right mix of CEO and COO, therefore, organizations need to consider both positions equally and review the mix regularly.

Again, a formal model helps to evaluate the rightness of a COO. In the book *Riding Shotgun: The Role of the COO* by Nathan Bennett and Stephen A. Miles, the authors detail seven reasons why an organization has a COO:

1. To provide daily leadership in an operationally intensive business
2. To lead a specific strategic imperative undertaken by management
3. To serve as a mentor to a young or inexperienced CEO (often a founder)
4. To balance or complement the strengths of the CEO
5. To foster a strong partnership at the top
6. To teach the business to the heir apparent to the current CEO
7. To retain executive talent that other firms may be pursuing[2]

For example, when Avon's board hired CEO Charlie Perrin, they saw Andrea as the heir apparent but felt she needed operations experience. Thus, reason 3 applied to the role Andrea played as COO—she was able to learn and grow and ready herself to assume the CEO position at some point in the future. There's ample precedent for this COO rationale—at ExxonMobil, Rex Tillerson transitioned smoothly to CEO after being Lee Raymond's number 2; the same is true of Colgate's Ian Cook moving into Reuben Mark's position and Tim Cook taking over for Steve Jobs at Apple.

Yet often, this transition doesn't go smoothly, or the combination of individuals is marked by tension and counterproductivity rather than synergy. That's the result of giving too little thought to the CEO-COO relationship. Following are four factors that create great CEO-COO relationships and contribute to organizational success:

- Role clarity between the two positions—unambiguous delineation of job responsibilities so that little or no overlap exists.

- Willingness of the CEO to mentor the COO and shift power and the responsibility from her shoulders to those of the heir apparent.

- A degree of trust and openness between the two individuals.

- The ability of the COO to accept being number 2 for a finite and reasonable period of time.

At Avon, the board told Charlie Perrin that he had to make Andrea his COO and groom her for his job. Unfortunately, most of the other factors that help a CEO-COO relationship were absent. Charlie didn't seem eager to mentor Andrea, and if they didn't distrust each other, neither were they particularly open or friendly. One Avon executive recalled that Andrea once held an operations meeting to which Charlie was not invited, but he showed up anyway, creating the sort of awkward, tense situation that neither person ever forgets. Furthermore, Andrea was not content to bide her time, and Charlie was in no hurry to leave his position—she was an ambitious 39-year-old, and he was only 52, with many years of work ahead of him. Andrea's charisma contrasted with Charlie's more straightforward leadership style. As skilled as he was operationally, he was not in Andrea's league when it came to putting on a show. Consequently, whenever they appeared together in internal meetings or when presenting to external groups, Andrea outshone Charlie. Invariably, he must have resented having a subordinate who dominated whatever room they appeared in together.

You would think, given this experience, that Andrea would have learned the importance of the four factors. Certainly the relationship between Andrea and her first COO, Susan Kropf, was terrific and served the organization well, but with Susan's impending retirement the board insisted on bringing in a high-potential backup to hedge against Andrea being poached. Liz Smith was hired in 2005 as VP and brand president and took on roles of increasing responsibility (she became the number 2 person in the company as its president in 2007) and drove the global centralization effort. She had her own coach and worked at transforming her image to meet the requirements of being the head of a company where style and charisma were important. But for all her efforts, she left after a few years to become CEO of Bloomin' Brands, Inc. Did Andrea do all she could to develop and coach Liz for the CEO role? Should Andrea have groomed another successor if she anticipated that Liz might leave for a CEO role elsewhere or if she and/or the board thought that Liz wasn't ready to take on the job? While these questions are difficult to answer, they point out how challenging the task can be for CEOs to develop their successors. Anne Mulcahy, former CEO of Xerox, did a great job of deliberately preparing Ursula Burns to take over, but this is often the exception rather than the rule. For one thing, there isn't always the time needed to coach and develop a successor. For another, CEOs may be psychologically averse to preparing an individual to replace them.

Looking back at the four factors, the primary one that wasn't met was the time frame. When Liz joined the company, she must have been aware that Andrea had intimated that she only wanted to be CEO of Avon for ten years—that would have meant that Liz would take over in 2008. But neither Andrea nor the board gave any indication that there would be a CEO change, so Liz must have felt she had to go elsewhere if she were to become a CEO.

Returning to the CEO-COO combination of Andrea and Susan, not only were the four criteria met, but Andrea and Susan established a rhythm to their relationship that benefited the company tremendously, one that seems to characterize all the best CEO-COO relationships. They respected and trusted one another and possessed complementary areas of expertise. Generally, top leaders have one of two tilts: to the visionary/strategic side or to the operations/execution side. Andrea tilted one way, Susan the other. It probably also helped that Susan was humble, with no ambition to become CEO. At one point, when Avon's fortunes were soaring, a major business publication wanted to profile Andrea as one of the best bosses. Andrea reportedly told the publication that she was not the best boss but that she and Susan together were the best boss together and that she wouldn't do the interview without Susan.

Some CEOs are too egotistical to admit that they can't do it all or are too threatened by a COO who possesses skills that they lack, or they bring in COOs who are reflections of themselves and don't bring critical new skills and perspectives to the table. Facebook CEO Mark Zuckerberg said it well when commenting on his hiring of COO Sheryl Sandberg: "There are people who are really good managers, people who can manage a big organization, and then there are people who are very analytic or focused on strategy. These two types don't usually tend to be the same person. I would put myself much more in the latter camp by hiring Sandberg."[3] He acknowledged, too, that he wasn't interested in tasks such as hiring and firing and political issues, and he was happy to turn all that over to Sandberg. Similarly, Andrea was perfectly happy to give Susan complete control over the tasks she didn't like to do and ones in which she lacked expertise.

At other high-level organizations, you'll find relationships similar to that of Andrea and Susan. Hewlett Packard's Meg Whitman says this about her COO, Bill Veghte, in a 2013 *Forbes* magazine interview: "Bill . . . and I have a very good complementary partnership. Having grown up in the enterprise, he knows it incredibly well and is deep from a technology perspective. I'm very good on strategy, market segmentation, communications and leading the charge."[4]

At IBM, CEO Lou Gerstner initially went it alone, without a COO. In preparing for his succession, however, he appointed Sam Palmisano as COO. Grooming an insider, a "native with a roadmap" was critical to Gerstner. He and Palmisano were an unlikely pair, given that the former was a hard-charging, classic command-and-control leader and the latter was more easygoing and enjoyed give-and-take. Despite these very different styles, Palmisano helped Gerstner be a better CEO, and

Gerstner groomed Palmisano to hit the ground running when he took over.

The late Steve Jobs and his COO, Tim Cook (now CEO), also had a great complementary relationship. Jobs was extraordinarily confident and design focused; Cook was less emotional and more analytical. While the jury is still out on Cook as CEO, there's no question that his operations and cost-controlling skills helped Jobs function as a highly effective leader—the right leader for Apple at the right time.

In Meg Whitman's *Forbes* interview, she said, "I try to figure out what I'm uniquely good at—and surround myself with people who are really good at what I'm not good at."[5] That's not a bad philosophy for every CEO to adopt.

For more specific advice, here are some questions organizations should ask themselves as they choose COOs and monitor CEO-COO relationships:

- Can you identify at least one specific role (of the seven listed earlier) that a prospective COO will play in your organization, or is a COO being chosen more because of a close relationship with the COO and/or because he or she is a mirror image of the CEO?
- Has a given individual taken on roles in the past that were complementary (to the CEO's strength)? Was this person successful in these roles? How do you envision these complementary skills being leveraged in combination?
- Do the CEO and COO play well together? That is, do they display mutual respect and trust? Is there a rhythm to their relationship, a sense that they are reflexively supportive of and responsive to each other?
- Is there animosity or resentment between the CEO and COO? Does the CEO act paranoid about the ambitions of the COO? Does the COO seem to chafe at being number 2 and resent the uncertainty about when she will be number 1?

CFOS: MORE THAN BOOK CLOSERS

There's a third member of the leadership team that impacts whether the CEO is the right leader at the right time, and it's often a position that is overlooked and underutilized. Typically, organizations have viewed CFOs as money guys (or gals) in the narrowest sense of the term. While "doing the books" is obviously an important job in any organization, that definition undersells the job. In a complex, volatile, global world, CEOs need their CFOs to be strategic partners.

To that end, consider a 2013 McKinsey study of 100 leading global companies that identified four critical CFO roles:

- Finance expert—The traditional numbers role and one that McKinsey found was best suited to a decentralized company where the priority is standardizing compliance and financial processes.
- Generalist—A broader approach to the job, one that often incorporates operations, marketing, and other disciplines. McKinsey determined this role was best suited to capital-intensive industries where operations are key.
- Performance leader—A transformational role and one highly useful in companies that require performance metrics.
- Growth champion—Given the current emphasis on growth strategies, it's not surprising that McKinsey found that this role represented 25 percent of new CFO hires. [6]

During Andrea's golden period as CEO, Avon was evolving from a holding company to a more global, integrated enterprise. Thus, there was a clear need for a finance expert to help upgrade and consolidate financial systems and processes and to improve margins by leveraging economies of scale and improving cash flow through reductions in inventory. CFO Bob Corti was a tremendously savvy finance professional, but he also served a broader role that encompassed the three other functions identified by McKinsey. He was known as Andrea's consigliore but also as the keeper of Avon's ethics. Throughout the organization, Bob had a reputation for speeches in which he urged employees to embrace "doing the right things when no one is watching." Though Bob was criticized in some quarters for not being tougher with Andrea and for not taking full control of the integration of worldwide financial resources, he did preside over double-digit growth and margin improvement. Bob fulfilled the role (financial) that was most critical to the company at the time while also meeting the demands of other roles when necessary.

In 2005, when the board replaced Corti with Chuck Cramb, the organization needed to accelerate the pace at which it integrated processes globally. More so than in the past, the CFO needed to be skilled at consolidating financial systems from multiple geographies as well as foreign exchange hedging (which had served Avon well in the past). In addition, Avon had to establish consistent and contemporary metrics to evaluate its business and make investment decisions as it changed and grew—especially in all the new foreign markets that were becoming the dominant source of revenue for the company. Thus, the finance and performance roles were key for the new CFO.

The board wanted a more contemporary CFO who brought a mix of finance skills and strategy to deal with the broader global issues Avon faced. In addition, the company had continued to flirt with potential acquisitions as a pathway to growth, and Cramb was an accomplished deal maker who appeared to have the targeted skill set as well as the strength to push back on Andrea when necessary. Cramb, however, had come from Gillette, a domestically focused, low-growth, capital-intensive organization. He was terrific at the generalist role, and one executive who worked with him suggested that he might have preferred being chief strategist over chief financial officer. During quarterly analyst calls, Chuck spent a lot of time discussing the strategy and sidestepping questions about margins and inventory management. Although he focused on expense management, as previously mentioned, SG&A

actually rose during his tenure as net income declined. In addition, the organization was beset with the ongoing bribery investigation and was in need of more rigorous FCPA training. Foreign exchange challenges, too, existed in many markets, and the infrastructure was crumbling. One former finance staff member said, "You had two captains at the helm and no one stoking the engines." At this point in its evolution, Avon could have used someone like Carol Tomé, Home Depot's CFO, who slowed down new store openings and chose to invest those resources in technology and training and rebuilding low morale.

While Cramb and Andrea seemed to work well together, his skills didn't match up well with the organization's changing objectives and needs during this phase of growth. This wasn't Cramb's fault as much as the board's and Andrea's—someone should have asked the right questions in the first place. Ultimately, the board should have been less impressed by pedigree and more concerned about what potential CFO would best be able to solve the financial issues besetting the company. Cramb arrived with a great deal of fanfare, and there's no question that he was a highly skilled, contemporary-minded financial professional. To some, however, he was a "deal guy" who was more concerned about facilitating a merger or acquisition than concentrating on other CFO responsibilities. But the board needed to focus on the financial skills that would be critical in that position during the next five years, and they seemed to have missed the mark.

To assess a CFO's ability to help the CEO be the right leader at the right time, conduct the following four-step analysis:

1. Determine whether the company is most in need of a finance expert, generalist, performance leader, or growth champion. Make this assessment based on what is the most critical issue the company faces now and is likely to face in the near future (i.e., declining productivity because of a culture that accepts competency and doesn't demand excellence or the need for a performance leader).

2. Identify which role a CFO is most comfortable playing and whether he or she possesses the skills and experience to play it well.

3. Analyze whether the CFO is equipped to play a new role as the organization evolves (i.e., Is the generalist ready and able to handle new and complex financial issues arising from a major acquisition?).

4. Compare the CEO's financial acumen with that of the rest of the team, identifying how a CFO's skills are complementary.

THE C-TEAM

Some senior leadership teams are much more effective than others, and the reasons for this usually have less to do with skills and more to do with the collaborative ability of all team members. At Avon, Andrea and her team meshed superbly during the first five or six years of her tenure. An esprit de corps existed; an ability to communicate well and work together effectively that was invaluable to the organization. The transparency and respect in the senior leadership meetings translated into open exchanges of ideas and information and a willingness to seek the best solutions, not the solutions that served a given faction's agenda.

In the latter years of Andrea's reign, the composition of this team was very different. It wasn't that this second group was any less experienced or skilled, but they lacked cohesion. They were a mixture of external hires from multinationals and veteran Avon executives, which created an us-versus-them atmosphere. As I've discussed, the Avon group suspected that the new group disdained the direct sales model and the overly nice culture of the company; the external hires felt like they were treated as outsiders and were never given credit for understanding the business.

I'm not suggesting that all members of C-teams should be best friends; I'm not even saying they have to like each other. A certain amount of creative tension can be productive, and you want a diverse representation so that a variety of points of view can be heard.

Too often, however, a leadership team is put together primarily (and sometimes only) based on the skills of the individual members. The team needs an expert in global management, someone who has strategic acumen, and someone with branding talent. Again, there's nothing wrong with any of this and a lot that's right about it, as you don't want to clone the CEO and have a surplus of identical skills and styles.

But these teams often are composed of at least a few ill-fitting pieces.

No doubt, you've been in meetings where two team members can't stand each other. Perhaps their personalities just clash. Perhaps they have different theories about how to run a business. Perhaps there is animosity from a past encounter. Whatever the reason, it's unlikely that two mismatched people will ever work well together, no matter how much coaching you give them.

Now consider what happens if, instead of just two people who can't work well together, you have five, or eight. During times of high stress and low performance, the tensions in the room, combined with the egos of top executives, form a combustible stew. For this reason, organizations need to evaluate fit when selecting the leadership team and when monitoring their performance. Admittedly, this is a tough factor to select for and measure. Nonetheless, it must be part of the conversation.

If the previous paragraph reminds you of the current (as of this writing) president and members of the opposition party, then you see the point I'm making. President Obama, like Andrea, was challenged by the aloof derailer. He has failed to reach across the table and help bridge the differences that divide Democrats and Republicans. It's not that he doesn't want to do this but rather that his aloof derailer gets in the way of doing it effectively. In Andrea's case, her pleaser derailer also came into play, in that she knew that if she cracked the whip and forced people to move away from their deeply held positions, they would resent it, and more to the point, they would resent her.

Finding ways to create high-functioning teams involving members who have different styles and perspectives is a challenge for boards and CEOs, and to meet this challenge, they should ask the following questions about their leadership team participants:

- When adding new members to the executive team, have these individuals been evaluated for more than the specific skills or the experience they bring? Have they been assessed for how they might fit with the existing team? Based on what you know about a given individual's personality and beliefs, is there anyone on the existing team with whom he or she might struggle?
- Is the leadership team plagued by two opposing factions (e.g., tea party Republicans versus left-leaning Democrats)? What is the source of the divisiveness, and has there been any effort to heal the wounds? Is it feasible that something can be done to overcome differences, or is it unlikely that the team can function at a high level of effectiveness? Is the CEO helping or hindering the continuation of these factions? What changes in his or her behavior need to be made to drive more cohesion?
- Does the senior team work as well as a unit today as it did a year ago? Three years ago? Five years ago? Is the problem that the composition of the team has changed? Or has the team remained the same but the organization has changed (and members don't work as well facing current challenges as they did when the environment was easier to deal with)? Is more formal team alignment work needed to ensure all are moving in the right direction?

It would be nice if all it took to have the right leader at the right time was a savvy CEO selection. But as I've learned over the years, other ingredients have to be present for this rightness to exist, from a highly collaborative senior leadership team to a COO who complements the CEO perfectly. Getting this mix of individuals right isn't always easy, but recognizing all the factors that should be in place facilitates the process.

EIGHT

CULTURE EATS STRATEGY FOR LUNCH

NEVER UNDERESTIMATE THE POWER OF CULTURE. WHEN I FIRST HEARD THE EXPRESSION that is this chapter's title, I joked about it with a colleague, a professor specializing in business strategy. It was only later, when I got to Avon, that I understood how true it was. Before I joined Avon, I worked at two large corporations—one in financial services, the other pharmaceutical—and their cultures failed to impress me. But Avon was different. More than one person referred to the culture there as "the special sauce."

Avon employees had a sense of purpose. Between the mission of women's empowerment and the relationship-driven, direct-selling model, people who worked there believed deeply in giving back to the community. Even years after leaving the company, people speak with great fondness of their experience there, and many are active in alumni groups.

Culture is a complex and critical component of leadership. Yet many leaders underestimate its impact or fail to deal effectively with it in conjunction with growth strategies and other business initiatives. As CEO Lou Gerstner said about IBM's culture during a period of transformation, "I came to see, in my time at IBM, that culture isn't just one aspect of the game—it is the game."[1]

Because Avon's culture was so powerful and distinctive and because that culture badly needed to evolve during Andrea's tenure, it provides a fascinating case study. Andrea recognized the need for cultural evolution and took steps to try and change it in tandem with implementation of new business policies and programs. In some respects, she was successful—but more broadly, culture ate strategy for lunch.

One of the biggest challenges for leaders charged with evolving their organizations is that the same characteristics that once made a company great can also derail key business objectives. Even when cultures need to evolve, changing them too quickly or radically can destroy the spirit of an organization. There are many fine lines leaders must walk when it comes to culture, so let's start out by exploring how culture connects business goals to organizational norms and environments.

CULTURE AS OPPORTUNITY OR OBSTACLE

Culture has many definitions, but for our purposes here, let's agree that it consists of a company's norms and values; it manifests itself in "the way things are done around here" and includes both the formal and informal rules of the game. In most established companies of at least moderate size, certain identifiable traits cut across geographic and functional boundaries. At the same time, subcultures can exist within departments or regional offices. For instance, a marketing or accounting culture may have distinct characteristics that aren't shared with the larger corporate culture. Similarly, the culture in a company's Hong Kong office may be different from that of the one in Paris.

Cultures aren't dictated from above, nor do they just mysteriously emerge. Instead, they arise as employees have common experiences and develop a shared view of their particular universe. Often, as the executive team figures out the best way to grow (i.e., organic versus acquisition), these methods become ingrained in the company's DNA. The problem is that when the external world changes, this internal world often remains the same. A large global energy company had a culture of great rigor and discipline, and in the past, this reflexive belief in slow but certain analytical processes helped them make wise investments that have greatly benefited their organization. Now, however, they are facing intense competition from smaller but more nimble competitors. They need to move faster and with greater agility, but their culture is an impediment.

Yet there is still great value in the global energy company's culture. To try and change it overnight would be disastrous. Rigor and discipline are valuable competencies, but they need to be moderated and leavened with new elements. The culture must evolve or it will become a serious liability as the business environment changes.

Another problem is the gap between appearance and reality. Companies may espouse certain cultural values and beliefs, but they aren't aligned with how employees behave. Enron is the best example of this disconnect. While Enron's leaders talked about how values such as excellence and integrity were ingrained in the organization, authors McLean and Elkind in their book *The Smartest Guys in the Room: The Amazing Rise and Scandalous Fall of Enron*, interviewed Enron employees and found that they characterized the culture with words such as cutthroat, arrogant, greed, and exploitation.[2]

As we'll see, Andrea and some of the others in Avon's leadership group recognized and valued the company's culture, yet they weren't always successful in evolving it to correspond to changing business realities. This is not an uncommon problem. For this reason, every organization should conduct a regular cultural assessment and then analyze environmental changes to see how their culture fits—or doesn't—with the external landscape. It may be that significant cultural evolution is required, or it may be sufficient to recast or contemporize. Here are six questions that every organization should ask about their cultures for a useful assessment:

1. What are three to seven common beliefs of employees—beliefs about the behaviors and skills that are rewarded, the attitudes

that are prized, the business philosophy that is espoused, the way people are treated by the organization, and so on?

2. What are the stories that people tell and retell throughout the company—war stories about organizational triumphs, tales about charismatic founders and current leaders, stories about failures? What are the themes of these stories—leadership, innovation, and so forth?

3. Where are the informal centers of power? How do "things get done around here"? Are there certain people, positions, or functions that wield the greatest power, and if so, why does this informal power grid exist (i.e., to circumvent a slow-moving bureaucracy)?

4. Who are the go-to people in the organization? Who are the individuals who are viewed as problem solvers and out-of-the-box thinkers? Who are the potential blockers or the ones who could derail change? Who are the ones who can break stalemates, resolve conflicts, and seize opportunities? Are they the individuals highest on the organizational chart, or are they the "old salts?" What are the communication channels? How is information transmitted, both formally and informally? Is the communication straightforward, or is it necessary to read between the lines? Is a lot of the information restricted by managerial level and function, or is it open to most if not all employees? Is there a lot of one-on-one communication, written versus verbal, meetings versus memos, and so on?

5. Who are the employees who are most respected, and why? Do they tend to be the organizational leaders or the managers on the front lines? What are the qualities most prized in these respected individuals?

Increasingly, organizations are recognizing that cultural assessments need to be prioritized. More than ever before, they see the connection between cultural norms and strategic goals. Google, for instance, conducts regular "pulse" surveys to measure aspects of their culture. Johnson & Johnson, whose culture is driven by its credo ("puts the needs and well-being of the people we serve first . . ."), has put credo challenges in place designed to help teams discuss what the credo means to them as well as encouraging behaviors that are credo-consistent. Recently, I worked with a European organization to ensure alignment between their strategy and the company's culture; they also want to communicate to the external world that how they treat their clients mirrors how they treat their employees.

Culture, then, isn't something to take for granted; it must be assessed and adjusted regularly, which requires a savvy leadership hand. Let's look at the culture change that Andrea attempted to put in place at Avon.

BUILDING A HIGH-PERFORMANCE CULTURE

When Andrea arrived at Avon, she found a strongly entrenched culture that valued direct selling, entrepreneurship, local independence, a family atmosphere, and had a suspicion of outsiders. The high-performance culture that Andrea hoped to create would require a relentless pursuit of vision, a performance-driven environment, and simple structures and core processes. Perhaps more significant from a cultural standpoint, achieving this high-performance culture would mean a shift from intuitive to fact-based leadership, from loose and varied processes to highly disciplined ones, from consensus decision making to clear accountabilities.

When Charlie Perrin was CEO, he tried to push the culture in this direction and was met with resistance from general managers around the world. They felt insulted and that corporate was trying to shove the change down their throats. When Andrea became CEO, she was more sensitive to their plight and empowered the HR group to facilitate the culture change. In one sense, facilitation meant translating the consultant-derived verbiage into specific behaviors that employees could enact. It also meant realigning the performance management and compensation systems so that they reinforced these behaviors. And finally, it meant that HR would coach Andrea to model these behaviors and refrain from blinking when she met with resistance.

Leadership modeling is far more important to cultural change than most people realize. Employees are watching everything leaders do and taking their cues from them. They are attuned to what leaders focus on and what they measure. They pay attention to how resources are allocated and when they're taken away. They notice who gets hired and promoted.

Academics often make cultural change sound easy, or at least linear. In fact, it's often nuanced, nonverbal, and indirect. Leaders can inadvertently sabotage the whole process by being inconsistent. For instance, they may say all the right things and create a terrific nine-step program to create a high-performance culture, but if the rewards system doesn't reinforce it, that creates a fatal disconnect.

Beyond creating alignment between culture-change goals and leadership behaviors, the sine qua non of the process is to secure engagement. When employees throughout an organization connect with the cultural changes, they internalize them, and their behaviors reflect these internalized messages. Avon's approach to cultural engagement was pioneering in certain ways, and while it wasn't always successful, it highlights certain truths about culture change and illustrates how to increase the odds of managing it effectively.

THE IMPLICATIONS OF CULTURE ON LEADERSHIP

Working with leadership development consultant Peter Cairo, Avon's HR executive group (of which I was a member) began an assessment of the company's leaders and the culture, designed to help Avon overcome leadership resistance to organizational changes. Using 360-degree feedback and two personality assessment instruments (the leadership derailers referenced in previous chapters) based on the Hogan Development Survey and Fundamental Interpersonal Relationship Orientation Inventory (FIRO-B), Avon intended to apply the results in coaching sessions and small teams to help leaders change their behaviors.

But the company also aggregated the results, and as an unintended but valuable byproduct, this work provided a fascinating analysis of Avon's culture, spotlighting the disconnect between cultural norms and implementation of the new operating model. A number of insights emerged from the assessment and from my observations at Avon and at other organizations. Following are some of the insights I have gleaned:

Cultural insight 1: Companies tend to select, whether deliberately or unconsciously, people (especially leaders) who fit the culture.

Some organizations, such as Google, overtly hire with certain traits and attitudes in mind to ensure people will flourish in the Google environment. Other organizations, like Avon, didn't actively seek new hires who fit the culture, but they did end up hiring people who displayed shared characteristics—especially in the leadership group. Some of these characteristics of the Avon culture included:

- An entrepreneurial, risk-taking spirit.
- Difficulty listening to others and accepting feedback and responsibility for mistakes.
- A preference for autonomy, resulting in silos.
- Selectivity in forming relationships; prioritizing relationships where there's a history over ones dictated by organization structure and hierarchy.
- Gravitating toward environments that are loose and open with few formal agendas and structured roles.
- Responding warmly to other people in ways that can be misread as cooperation and alignment.

When Avon disseminated the results of this cultural inventory, it sparked plenty of informal conversation. The dialogues were spontaneous, not the result of formal meetings or memos. People saw the gaps between the way leaders at Avon behaved and the organizational changes that had been mandated, and they wanted to talk about it.

Cultural insight 2: Creating awareness of the gap between cultural behavior and organizational change can bring the issue out in the open, making it easier to deal with.

At Avon, the cultural assessment highlighted how the traits that had helped the company succeed in the past were proving to be obstacles in executing its new strategy. The assessment found that Avon was:

- Attempting to centralize certain functions and decisions with a profile of leaders who sought autonomy and valued entrepreneurship.
- Focusing on process, structure, discipline, and rules of the road, with a profile of leaders who perhaps viewed rules as made to be broken.
- Attempting to leverage economies of scale and best practices with a profile of leaders who would rather work independently in their own silos and were not naturally collaborative.

The dissonance between the existing cultural norms and the required ones was striking. Identifying the specific reasons for the dissonance was a great first step, but creating the cultural engagement that would pave the way for the new plan would be an even bigger step.

Cultural insight 3: The cultural discussion must unfold without defensiveness.

How do you tell organizational leaders that they need to start following the rules or that they have to get out of their silos and collaborate more effectively? At Avon, these leaders were proud and accomplished, having helped to build a large, profitable company. In the past, their cultural preferences had matched the business strategy. To accuse them of being out of touch with the times or to suggest that they were sabotaging the company's business objectives would have invited acrimonious debate that led nowhere or, even worse, feigned acceptance of a new approach while secretly resisting it. Instead, the HR group placed the discussion in the context of current behavioral patterns and the types of behaviors or new patterns required to execute the new strategies and operating model. This way, instead of insulting leaders or disparaging their past accomplishments, the HR executives kept conversations focused on the behaviors that were essential for productive and profitable organization change.

Cultural insight 4: It's better to focus on cultural evolution than cultural change.

This may seem like semantics, but evolution connotes slow and organic movement while change suggests speed and difficulty. At Avon, Andrea didn't impose cultural change by edict but implemented a gradual strategy. It began with formal and informal dialogues about cultures, moved toward identifying a set of actions that were consistent with cultural goals, and took shape as HR helped leaders develop new routines to replace existing ones. The dialogues were especially useful, as leaders were able to articulate strengths of the culture that helped achieve success in the past but would also be necessary for success in the future. At the same time, they came to understand how these strengths could also be liabilities, especially in the clash of centralized and decentralized processes.

These discussions were truly evolutionary, in that the leaders themselves were helping to find the right blend of old and new and create a path to move toward this blend. They were able to identify the specific policies and philosophies that needed to change and the ones that needed to be retained. Perhaps even more important, leaders admitted that it would be difficult to change individually and collectively; it was important because it allowed them to concentrate on a manageable set of behaviors (rather than more sweeping and immediate changes). An informal bargain was reached in which participants in the dialogues agreed that the senior team would oversee this evolutionary cultural process and call them if their behaviors reverted back to the old cultural model rather than the blended one that everyone had agreed would serve the company best.

Cultural insight 5: A common language is crucial to facilitating cultural evolution.

Early on, a consultant had recommended organizational changes not unlike those Avon eventually adopted. But the consultant's language felt foreign, so Avon's leaders had to find a way to talk about what needed to change without feeling threatened or defensive. The process I just described helped people own the changes they needed to make. By talking through their hopes and fears and understanding how essential it was for changes to be made, they embraced cultural change and became conscious of modeling the behaviors that would help make it happen.

THE CULTURAL BALANCE

The two keys to successful cultural evolution are finding a way to retain the best of the old while embracing the best of the new and managing the pace of culture change so that it fits the needs of the organization. Many companies can make small changes with relative ease, but when they're required to make more significant changes—and to make them faster—the balance between old and new is upset. In Andrea's first six years at Avon, cultural evolution occurred at a measured pace. While she encountered some resistance to changes she was encouraging—more collaboration and fewer silos, universal adoption of best practices rather than following instinct, and using local tactics—the majority of leaders tried to change their behaviors so they were aligned with the new organizational strategy. But when earnings hit a wall in 2005 and costs increased, more radical evolution was necessary. Culturally speaking, Andrea wanted her people to embrace a globally integrated network, to be more analytical in their assessments and decision making and to prioritize execution. This cultural shift would help make the strategic de-layering and shift to a global matrix structure more viable.

In this situation, it's always tempting to bring in new people who possess not only the needed skills but also the culturally correct attitudes and behaviors to replace people with incorrect attitudes and behaviors. This may be the fastest, most effective way to create a desired cultural shift, but it comes with a warning.

Cultural insight 6: Hiring from the outside can help change the culture but at a major cost to the business.

At IBM when Lou Gerstner embarked on cultural change, he recognized the danger of bringing in a flood of outsiders, even though many observers expected him to do exactly that. He said at the time, "If necessary, I will bring in outsiders, but you will first get a chance to prove yourself. . . . Everyone starts with a clean slate. Neither your successes nor failures in the past count with me."[3]

Andrea, though, chose a different path, in large part because she felt she lacked the internal expertise necessary to drive the changes she wanted to make. In 2005, eight of Avon's 13 executive committee members were new to the company, as were 35 percent of the company's top 125 managers. A significant percentage of these new hires came from Kraft, a consumer-packaged goods company, suggesting that the company intended to move away from direct selling, in the direction of P&G or Unilever. Though Andrea didn't intend this message to be sent, there was obvious tension in meetings when both insiders and outsiders were present. This tension increased as longtime leaders with direct-selling expertise were forced out to make room for new people, the implicit message being that the insiders had messed things up and the outsiders had to come in and fix it. A former IT manager said the gossip in the corridors was that HR had decreed, "If you were here longer than 10 years, that must mean you are not that good."

But the biggest and most devastating cultural shift was the sudden perceived decree that headquarters knew best, and the individual markets must trust in corporate. The entrepreneurial, locally independent operation was no more. An Avon former senior leader said, "It used to be that the staff's role was to support the line. With the power shifting to the corporate functions, it evolved to the line supporting the staff."

All these moves conspired to diminish the importance and power of the Avon representative. And these representatives were the heart of Avon. For years, the company was known for empowering women with earnings opportunities and beauty at value prices. While Andrea didn't intend to diminish these representatives, that was the effect of bringing in so many new people and creating a centralized system with one-size-fits-all products and processes. One new Avon leader, hired from a packaged goods company, said in a tense meeting, "I want to love her [the representative] less and pay her more." Though there was logic to this approach, it subtly conveyed the message that even though the representative might get paid more, the company no longer valued her as it once had; she was no longer an essential member of the family. As a result, they didn't sell as much and they didn't sell as hard as they had in the past.

It wasn't that Andrea was wrong to try to change Avon's culture; it had to change. It's also possible that bringing in outsiders was essential because of the expertise Avon's top people lacked. But the fallout was not worth the minor gains achieved.

Cultural insight 7: Bringing together discipline with entrepreneurship creates a balance that helps evolve a culture successfully.

Unfortunately, Avon was never able to achieve this balance as its culture evolved. Rather than toggling nimbly between the discipline of centralized systems and processes to the entrepreneurial approach of the representatives, Avon appeared to favor the former over the latter. It was an unbalanced approach to reform, and one that the company struggles with to this day.

Looking back, it's possible that cultural evolution could have been successful if accompanied by other moves—such as the ones management guru Jim Collins suggested when Andrea asked him to speak at Avon's annual World Wide Management Conference held in 2004 of the most senior 100 leaders. Before agreeing to speak, he invited Andrea and Susan to his lab in Colorado to determine if they were in agreement on the theme of his talk: how combining a culture of discipline and an ethic of entrepreneurship creates superior performance. Collins wanted to allay fears that discipline did not equal bureaucracy by focusing conference attendees on discipline of thought and providing consistent frameworks for action. Although Jim's theme resonated with conference attendees, Avon could never negotiate the right balance between these two requirements. They either swung to one side or the other.

A TO-DO LIST FOR EVOLVING A CULTURE

I would be the last person to suggest that cultural evolution is easy, but I do believe it proceeds more smoothly if you know what to do—and what not to do. Most CEOs embark on this objective with little experience leading an evolution and often not much good advice. Typically, they face the same mandate as Andrea—changing the culture without destroying what makes the company special to its employees and customers. While this is a daunting task, it is by no means an impossible one.

From Andrea's experiences at Avon, as well my own consulting and research, I've identified several key tasks that any organization can undertake to further its cultural evolution:

- Make a long-term commitment of leadership time and energy. Gerstner put it well when he said, "I knew it would take at least five years. . . . I had to commit to thousands of hours of personal activity to pull off the change."[4] Former Kodak CEO, George Fisher, seconded this opinion as he looked back at Kodak and its culture: "Kodak is a very polite culture and people don't confront disagreement. . . . I didn't recognize it early enough. I should have spent a lot more time upfront on the culture inertia."[5] I'm not sure Andrea recognized how much of a commitment her strategy would be. It was not until 2005, when the financial situation became problematic, that she fully committed to remaking the culture, and by then it was almost too late. In fact, Andrea's inherent optimism probably prevented her from making an accurate assessment of how much time it would take to reconstruct the culture. CEOs and other top leaders often underestimate not only how much time this type of change will require but also to what extent employees in their organization take their cues from top management. A CEO who is consistent over time in his statements and actions and who sets a realistic time frame is most likely to have a positive impact on evolving that culture.
- Be clear on what the organization's culture is and what makes it unique. This isn't as obvious as it may sound. The new CEO who has been on the job for less than a year may not yet get it. Even more veteran employees may never have given much thought to the culture or spent time trying to articulate it clearly. Recognizing and honoring the things that make a

company unique is a good starting place for cultural evolution. Armed with this awareness, a CEO is less likely to advocate changes that trample on this legacy. Equally important, this awareness helps leaders recognize what elements should be preserved rather than changed.

When Anne Mulcahy became CEO of Xerox in 2001, she took over an organization near bankruptcy and a culture that many observers thought should be destroyed and rebuilt. Instead, she recognized that Xerox had a long and proud cultural tradition (she had worked for the company for 27 years) and decided to remind employees of the principles and values that had served the company well for a long time. These Xerox-centric principles and values struck a chord with many employees, revived morale, and releveraged a deeply loyal work force.

- Lead with the external, and the internal will follow. Concentrate first on communicating changes in the external environment, such as new customer requirements, that are driving the need for cultural evolution. When people understand the strategic context mandating cultural evolution, they are much more likely to embrace it.
- Detail the from-to cultural journey. Everyone from entry-level employees to the senior team needs specifics about where we are today (the from) and where we need to be (the to) and what will be different. Vague expressions about the need for more innovation or risk-taking mindsets won't cut it. Instead what is needed is a list of specific behaviors that will further the innovative goals. In addition, create opportunities for discussion about the from-to specifics, ranging from one-on-one conversations to team dialogues. Lou Gerstner would ask IBM employees to visualize what it would look like to have the "wind at our backs." It's also important to define what the from-to will look like in different parts of the world. Innovative behaviors

in China may take a different form than ones in Russia or the United States. The more specific you are about how the culture needs to evolve and the more it's tailored to a given audience, the better the outcome. It's especially important for the senior team to be aligned around the from-to model and the required behaviors. Detailing the journey and leadership modeling of the right behaviors start the process of cultural change, but it takes time and consistency to achieve it.

- Clarify and celebrate aspects of the culture that need to be preserved and aspects that once were crucial but no longer are. This isn't about denigrating the past and cheerleading for the future. Instead, the key is instilling pride in what the company represents—even in the parts of the culture that no longer are relevant—and focusing on what parts need to be sustained and how they will be sustained. Culture is complex, and it helps people to tease out aspects of the culture that have ceased to be useful and other cultural components that are essential for future growth.

    Marissa Mayer, Yahoo's CEO, felt that the organization had lost its collaborative edge, so when she came in she removed the partitions between cubicles to create more open space for dialogue. She also provided free food in the cafeteria (à la Google) to encourage more sharing. Finally, and most controversially, she enacted a ban on telecommuting to facilitate face-to-face interactions.

- Develop your stump speech around the cultural evolution. Perhaps most famously, GE's Jack Welch was brilliant at delivering the message for change at every opportunity using key words and phrases. Leaders make it a habit to reinforce the need for reshaping the culture, choosing quick but memorable ways of talking about it in a variety of settings. Repetition pays off, inculcating the reasons why evolution is imperative. Using symbols and stories, too, can make the message more memorable. When Southwest Airlines CEO Herb Kelleher took a pay cut when the airline industry was experiencing tough times, that voluntary reduction stood as a symbol for adopting a more austere, self-sacrificing mentality.

- Create positive reinforcement for cultural evolution. Performance management, incentives, and awards are just some of the common organizational tools that can be used to encourage people to evolve the culture through their work behaviors. Peer recognition programs can encourage collaboration and break down the silos.

- Keep it simple, and start small. Cultural evolution can feel overwhelming. Therefore, if you give people an accessible target in terms of behavioral change or if you create a memorable slogan that can guide their efforts, it makes cultural evolution doable in employees' minds. At Southwest, their slogan, "Employees first, then customers, then shareholders," made the cultural gestalt easy to grasp and execute. Leaders could develop programs and policies around these cultural priorities.

Finally, keep in mind that leaders are the guardians of the culture. As such, they need to constantly maintain their cultural consciousness, even when it seems less important than the daily business decisions they confront, such as dealing with a lawsuit or pursuing a growth opportunity for the company. It's the rare company that isn't in need of at least some cultural evolution as their business strategies and objectives change. To maintain a culture-centric mindset, leaders should routinely ask themselves how they're spending their time, who they're promoting (and not promoting), what topics they regularly discuss during meetings, their attitudes toward veteran employees if they're relatively new arrivals (or their attitudes toward new people if they're veterans). Leaders shape the culture by their attitudes and actions, and doing this consciously, rather than inadvertently, can save a world of trouble and misunderstanding.

NINE

WHAT'S GENDER GOT TO DO WITH IT?

AVON WAS A LEARNING LABORATORY FOR WOMEN AND LEADERSHIP. FEW LARGE, GLOBAL organizations had as many women in top positions as Avon. Fewer still provided women with the opportunity to stretch their leadership muscles, free of the constraints that sometimes exist in male-dominated cultures.

Andrea's triumphs and challenges at Avon, too, are of particular relevance to women who occupy top corporate jobs. In many ways, Andrea was the quintessential female CEO. She found the sweet spot between the iron maiden stereotype at one extreme and the maternal leadership style at the other. Her fall is also a good starting point for a discussion about why female CEOs or other female senior leaders might fail.

While this book is written in the belief that both Andrea's and Avon's stories contain valuable lessons for both men and women, I would be remiss if I didn't address the distaff side of leadership in this chapter. It is impossible to imagine a man leading Avon to such astonishing success as Andrea did. Her strategic insight and ability to motivate and inspire staff and female representatives around the world was extraordinary. It is also difficult to see a male CEO's failings played out in the public and prolonged in the way that Andrea's were. For these reasons, this chapter is designed to give all leaders insights about women in leadership roles and to offer women some specific strategies for maximizing their effectiveness in these roles.

First, however, I'd like to put Andrea's impact on other women leaders into perspective by answering two questions that might have occurred to you, and then comparing Andrea's style to another famous woman leader more than 400 years ago.

A QUEEN, BUT NOT A QUEEN BEE

In my interviews for this book, many of the women I interviewed asked two questions that I've thought a lot about:

Did gender have anything to do with Andrea's fall from grace?

Did Andrea's ultimate bad end at Avon serve as a black mark for other aspiring female leaders?

To the former, I would say probably not. I think Andrea did receive more media criticism than a male leader would have in the same situation, but that may have been due to the amount of praise she received earlier for her role in Avon's success. There is often a media backlash against people who have risen far and fast. In fact, Andrea's gender probably bought her more time in the job than a man would have had, given the problems that surfaced during the last few years of her time at Avon. She was an iconic female leader heading a company whose customers were women, an inspirational as well as an aspirational figure. It was not easy for the board to push her out. It's fair to say that it probably would have been easier for the board to get rid of a male leader in her position.

Regarding the second point, I don't think her fall hurt other women leaders. If she had burned out during her first few years on the job, it might have been a problem. But her tremendous success for the majority of her time as CEO more than counteracted the effect of the mistakes she made at the end.

Andrea's experience at Avon says a lot about other gender and leadership issues—ones that go beyond the old fears of glass ceilings and bias. I have had the opportunity to work with a wide variety of women leaders besides Andrea, including Karen Katen, former vice chairman of Pfizer; Susan Baer, former director of aviation for the Port Authority of New York and New Jersey; and Sheri McCoy, formerly of Johnson & Johnson and current Avon CEO. What I've learned is that gender is always an issue when it comes to leadership, but never in quite the same way. Each of the women I just mentioned brought different perspectives, experiences, and leadership styles to their jobs. Though their gender had an impact on their leadership approach and effectiveness, the impact was different for each of them. Susan Baer strived to build a family-oriented work environment with a focus on the whole person. Karen Katen was tough as nails in a budget meeting but was collegial in less-structured business settings—she was happy to join coworkers for drinks after work.

I'm reminded of a book I read years ago in graduate school, Rosabeth Moss Kanter's *Men and Women of the Corporation*, with its descriptions of various roles women assumed in the workplace: mother, seductress, pet, and iron maiden.[1] While I'm sure that women do assume some of these roles now, just as they did then (Kanter's book dates back to the 1970s), I also believe it's critical to take these gender-based descriptions with a grain of salt. Queen bee, for instance, recently reemerged as a popular term used to describe women leaders who are seen as imperious and absolute rulers.

Although I have called Andrea a beauty queen, I've done so because it was an apt description for her glamour and the industry she ruled, not because I found her to be a domineering boss. In fact, she was just the opposite in many ways. Not only wasn't she bossy, but she tried to serve as a role model for other women. She didn't want them to be worker bees forever; she hoped to elevate them to leadership positions—the leadership development program Andrea initiated at Avon was excellent. She helped shape the culture so that it was highly supportive of other women, modeling and endorsing behaviors that called for a work-life balance.

But Andrea was queenlike in certain ways, in that she carried herself with the grace and aura of a true lady. In fact, she was very much a modern-day, business equivalent of Queen Elizabeth I. Consider that both Queen Elizabeth and Andrea had clear, compelling visions—the queen for the power of England and Andrea for the power of Avon as a woman's empowerment organization. Both Andrea and the queen created fierce loyalty among their employees and subjects in large part because they favored making requests rather than issuing commands. Both of them dressed to the nines and projected an aura that carried them forward. Both rose to power early in their careers, and both were skilled at making powerful, motivating speeches to rally their constituencies and launch bold strategies.

I find the parallels between the two women fascinating in large part because it helps us understand how the qualities that make women effective leaders are timeless. There are many books about the different leadership styles of queens: Catherine the Great, Queen Victoria, Queen Isabella of Spain. Some women like Andrea possess a royal aura that is by turns charming, mesmerizing, motivating, and inspiring. But this royal style is only one of many available to women leaders, and the environment at Avon allowed many different styles to flourish.

THE IDEAL OF EQUALITY AND THE REALITY

I cannot envision an organization that is more receptive to women leaders than Avon. That said, I don't want to give the false impression that Avon was or is a paradise for every woman leader. As we all know, bad bosses aren't confined to one gender. Avon has had its share of less than stellar women managers, and they can make life difficult for both the men and the women with whom they work. A few women I interviewed were quick to remind me that sometimes policies related to gender were inconsistently applied and that inappropriate sexual advances occurred. One woman even related a story about her female manager giving her "the talk"—the lecture about how, at some point, she would have to choose between her career and her family.

What's different about Avon, though, is that it was, and remains the company for women; and since Andrea's CEO appointment, it's been run by women. Before Andrea's time, like a lot of other companies, it was slow to embrace the notion of gender equality. In the mid-1970s, the company appointed Pat Neighbors as its first female vice president. In one of her first executive staff meetings, she went from man to man at the table and complimented each of them on his tie, his shirt, his shoes, his hair. After she concluded her compliments, she noted that this was how each Avon male district manager began his meetings with female sales representatives.

A new era began when Jim Preston became CEO and made a commitment to name a woman CEO as his successor and also bring more women and minorities on board in executive positions. As a result, the company became known as a place where women could get ahead. Perhaps just as significantly, it began attracting what one former Avon woman executive termed "a special type of man." These men didn't feel threatened by women in power. In fact, they not only liked working for and with women but were committed to Avon's mission of empowering women.

When Andrea became CEO, one of her goals was to make Avon a great place for working mothers, and she implemented flexible work schedules for both sexes that made it easier for parents to take care of their kids. While other organizations give a lot of lip service to being mom-friendly, it was often not reflected in their actual policies. Andrea modeled behaviors that didn't just tolerate mothers but valued them. There's a story of the time Andrea was on a GE Board conference call on her son's birthday when her son came running into the room where she was talking and yelled, "This Scooby-Doo is the wrong color! I want the dark brown color, not the light brown color!" The board members heard his demand, and for years after that, they would ask Andrea, "So, dark or light brown Scooby-Doo?"[2] Andrea made it clear that moms have responsibilities that they should not be embarrassed about or avoid because of work situations; moms were encouraged to leave meetings if they had a child's event they wanted to attend.

Andrea's fellow GE board member Shelly Lazarus, then CEO of Ogilvy Mather Worldwide, told a story that captures the attitude that Shelly, Andrea, and a relatively small number of other pioneering women fostered: "A woman confided to me about 'sneaking out of the office' to go to her child's play, and I said, 'Stop right there! I have never snuck out of any place. I walk right down the center hall, and if somebody doesn't like it, too bad.'"[3]

Avon wasn't a perfect place for women, but it probably came closer than any other organization I had observed. People were conscious of gender equality and tried to live by it in all aspects of corporate life, whether it involved hiring decisions, pay, or work policies. That consciousness helped minimize bias and attracted both male and female managers who tried to treat people fairly. It also allowed women to lead authentically, not just Andrea, but Susan Kropf, Christina Gold, Liz Smith, Sheri McCoy, and many others.

SUCCESS AND FAILURE IN LEADERSHIP ROLES

Andrea never took Avon's motto, "the Company for Women," for granted. She wanted to stimulate discussions around women and success, and one of the best ways she found to do it was by launching the Avon Women's Leadership Forum. This was a two-day meeting of the sixty most senior women in the organization worldwide. The purpose of the forum was to understand the unique challenges confronting Avon's female leaders and develop actions to address them. For the meeting's agenda, Catalyst, a nonprofit organization that works to expand opportunities for women in business, allowed Avon to tailor their survey regarding female leaders' challenges to focus on company objectives. One of the key findings was that Avon needed to identify high-potential women early in their careers to give them the global exposure and game-changing assignments that help leaders develop. The logic behind this conclusion was that early on, women find it easier to take on these assignments (because children are younger and there are less issues about changing schools and abandoning friendships, and spouses have greater flexibility in their work schedules).

Avon also discovered that it needed to provide women with more support (coaching, training, and other resources) to increase their odds of success in these challenging assignments. For instance, Avon appointed a woman executive from Poland to be the general manager of Thailand, and in their rush to fill the post, they failed to provide her with cross-cultural training or much support of any kind. Unsurprisingly, the Thai office found her leadership style to be overly directive, and she grew concerned that her direct reports refused to push back with their own opinions.

Avon collected a lot of statistical data about factors that influence women's effectiveness in leadership roles, especially in general manager roles where taking on increased responsibility can be challenging (i.e., because they are the only senior women in a given market or because they're balancing family duties with work). Based on these data, as well as other organizational studies, five points emerged as essential to help women managers succeed:

1. *Ensure that women have access to the organization's game-changing assignments and give them sooner rather than later.* Gender bias can often play out subtly in what work is valued in the organization. "Research indicates that organizations tend to ignore or undervalue behind-the-scenes work (building a team, avoiding a crisis), which women are more likely to do, while rewarding heroic work, which is most often done by men."[4] The solution:

Organizations making the effort to understand the critical assignments that build capabilities for more senior roles and what the current challenges and assumptions are for moving women into those roles. Talent planning systems need to be established and focused on young high potentials, and they should make sure both men and women receive opportunities for cross-functional and global assignments. This means first-line managers must learn how to assess and develop talent so that more women with leadership abilities have the chance to be funneled into cross-functional training programs. More than that, it means that the organization needs to encourage these managers to take a star marketing performer and move her laterally into operations. Andrea would have benefited from this lateral move early in her career. This is the only way that some women will be able to escape the functional stereotypes they labor under ("She's great at marketing but doesn't have the head for the business stuff"). Finally, many large multinational organizations have moved to more transparent talent planning systems, where the criteria for high potentials is internally publicized, as are those game-changing assignments and the process for how to apply for them.

2. *Encourage women to seize stretch assignments.* One of the positive messages of Facebook's COO and women's leadership advocate, Sheryl Sandberg in *Lean In* is that women need to raise their hands when big opportunities come along. Men are often brought up to take reasonable risks; women are sometimes brought up to play it safe. Andrea's success would not have been possible if she had looked at the Avon job and said to herself, "I'm too young. I don't have any CEO experience, and I've never run a business before." She grabbed the opportunity and ran with it, and more women need to adopt this same attitude. Early on in her career, IBM CEO Virginia Rometty turned down an opportunity to take on additional responsibility by moving to an

unfamiliar functional area, figuring she lacked the experience to take on the position. When she talked about her decision with her husband, he said, "Do you think a man would have ever answered the question that way?" Rometty said, "What it taught me was that you have to be very confident—even though you're so self-critical inside about what it is you may or may not know."[5]

3. *Make sure women receive candid feedback, even if the conversations are difficult.* Early on, Avon conducted an analysis of performance reviews and found that men were tougher on other men than they were on women. I've found that both men and women often have difficulty giving direct feedback, and in today's meeting-laden environment neither sex spends as much time coaching as is needed. So the upshot is that women often don't receive the unadulterated feedback they require to learn and grow. Former Xerox CEO and turnaround leader Anne Mulcahy said that she was not hesitant to coach CEO candidate Ursula Burns to become more patient.[6] As a coach, I know that it's not easy for most leaders to give as well as receive feedback, but it's absolutely necessary. More than that, coaches and bosses must communicate how a given woman is perceived and how it is impacting her ability to achieve results. For instance, on a number of occasions I've had to tell women I'm coaching that they need to be better self-promoters or that they're too brash or that they need to be more self-assertive or that their political naïveté is hurting them. Some of this feedback may confirm traditional workplace gender stereotypes—female leaders get feedback that they need to be tougher/stronger (like a man) or that they have to soften up (because they've been overreacting to show everyone how tough they are). Some women also may receive contradictory feedback that they need to be tougher on staff but at the same time they are setting the bar too high. Many companies are implementing leadership development programs for women

to have a safe place to discuss their feedback, compare notes, and understand what success looks like for both genders in their organization and decide on the best actions to take individually and collectively. In most of these programs, the focus is more about purpose-driven leadership and the clarity with which leaders understand and articulate their overall mission and how they will lead to achieve it. As an example, Andrea was clear that her leadership purpose was doing something that helped and empowered women worldwide. She set out to do it with an authentic style that leveraged what she was good at and shored up her flat sides. She solicited feedback and wanted to understand perceptions of her effectiveness, but she did not let these perceptions of what she needed to do differently define her. For example, she knew she had to be tougher. She made conscious choices (at least some of the time) about what tough would look like given her personality and her values.

4. *Provide sponsorship as well as mentorship.* Mentors help to prepare individuals for those next jobs. Sponsors make it happen. Many women are mentored, but few are sponsored. Mentors are terrific, and Andrea had several who provided her with valuable support and advice. But sponsorship can give women an active boost to get a plum position within an organization. Claire Farley, a former Chevron senior executive now with KKR, put it this way: "A sponsor is someone influential who will pound the table for you."[7] Women need to get past their reluctance to promote themselves and ask for help in getting the jobs they want, and organizations need to ensure women have access to the networks, forums, and conversations that can open doors. Christina Gold, former President and CEO of the Western Union Company, as well as a former Avon executive, described the political skills women may lack and that sponsors can facilitate: "You need to make friends, alliances, and be shrewd and figure out where the power structure is and who's controlling the beat of

the organization. You have to figure out the players and how to insert yourself . . . and know your friends and enemies."

5. *Organizationally, leaders must also raise awareness about some of the subtle bias that still exists.* For example, I was coaching a manager, and we were reviewing the performance of each of his team members and how he had given each of them feedback about what they needed to do differently—feedback that was guiding their performance improvement. I asked him if he had had those same types of conversations with his female staff. He had not, explaining that it was easier to have these conversations with the men because they were "like him." He sometimes got together with them after work and over beers to discuss these issues. In effect, he was mentoring his male staff much more effectively than his female staff, even though that wasn't his conscious intent.

EVOLVING STYLES

We're not that far removed from a time when women leaders were seen as either tough cookies or sweet things, stern taskmasters or glamorous lightweights. In 1977, Katherine Graham of the *Washington Post* became the first female CEO of a Fortune 500 company, and in 1986, Linda Wachner took over as the CEO of Warnaco, and a magazine referred to her as among the seven "roughest, toughest, most intimidating bosses." Jill Barad, former CEO of Mattel, was better known for her Barbie-like wardrobe than her business results. When Andrea became CEO of Avon in 1999, though, things were changing. Other women were embracing leadership styles that had little to do with the stereotypes, based on their authentic personalities and values. On Avon's board alone, there were two women leaders with distinct styles. Brenda Barnes made no bones about putting her family first, and her low-key, no spotlight, consensus-building approach made her the highly effective first female CEO of PepsiCo, North America, though she eventually stepped down to spend more time with her family (seemingly stunned by all the attention her decision received). Though Ann Moore, chairman and CEO of Time Inc., had a quiet, results-driven style, she relished the spotlight and the fascinating people she met when she oversaw *People* and *Time* magazines. Both Brenda and Ann tried to achieve a balance of work and family, as well as do the work that inspires them.

Andrea was aware of how women in the corner office were perceived, and one of her most valuable contributions was being true to herself as a leader. Though she was beautiful, she didn't bat her eyelashes or wear revealing outfits. Though she possessed an inner toughness, outwardly she was kind and friendly. Despite the research at the time that suggested that some people didn't take pretty women CEOs seriously and other research that indicated nice women were perceived as soft, Andrea turned beauty and kindness into leadership assets. She adhered to values that her parents had helped her develop, and her charisma was not an act but arose from her personality. By being authentic, then, Andrea demonstrated that women could create their own style that ran counter to expectations. It was a tremendously effective style for six years, and when it ceased to be as effective as it had been, she was able to adjust it so that it was a better fit with the situation in which she found herself. Andrea never became inauthentic but recognized that agility in style was just as crucial as agility in strategy and other disciplines. As she adapted her style, she remained a caring, charismatic leader, but she also developed a tougher, more bottom-line-driven mentality.

In fact, women's leadership styles have evolved so much in recent years that it is now almost as difficult to stereotype women's leadership personas as it is men's. Given the diversity of potentially effective styles, organizations should learn from Andrea's example and do the following:

- Encourage high-potential women leaders to identify and
  cultivate their broader leadership purpose, as well as develop

their authentic style. In addition, provide them with HR assistance and coaching so that they recognize the traits that are natural to them and learn how to apply them in leadership situations.

- Discourage putting on an act. Stereotypes still exert influence on women. They believe that they need to be tough as nails to gain acceptance; they think they have to be nurturing in order to gain commitment from their people. Through one-on-one conversations and training, organizational leaders should communicate that authenticity is prized and artificiality is not.

- Promote situational agility. Boards, HR professionals, and coaches should help women leaders adapt their styles to changing situations. Agility is a buzzword in organizations for a reason—a volatile environment demands that leaders become tougher or softer, more decisive, more patient, and so on. Though this is a gross generalization, women tend to be more flexible than men. Therefore, they should capitalize on their capacity to learn, grow, and change to meet evolving organizational requirements.

THE DOUBLE-BIND DILEMMA

In 2007, Catalyst issued a research report titled "The Double-Bind Dilemma for Women in Leadership: Damned if You Do, Doomed if You Don't."[8] The report refers to how women often don't know if they should present a tough front to their organizational worlds or if they should adopt a softer, more feminine stance. Hillary Clinton, for instance, was initially criticized as being overly assertive, but when she softened her image and began being more emotive in her talks, she was criticized for being inauthentic. In her memoir, Carly Fiorina notes that she was often referred to as a "bimbo" or "bitch."[9] When I was at Pfizer, Vice Chairman Karen Katen was perceived as not tough enough by the board and was passed over in 2001 for CEO in favor of Hank McKinnell, whose style was much harder edged. An analyst noted at the time, "Hank is the right guy for the job. He's got a toughness about him."[10] After falling earnings and internal strife, McKinnell resigned in 2006.

At Johnson & Johnson, Sheri McCoy, who became Avon's CEO, was passed over for the top job there in favor of Alex Gorsky. At the time, Johnson & Johnson was facing numerous challenges, including congressional hearings, and the board seemed to want a CEO who presented a tough, polished front. On the one hand, Alex had come up through sales and had a West Point background. Sheri, on the other hand, was collaborative, humble, and down-to-earth, and while she too could be tough, she exhibited that quality in a more subtle way.

Despite these negative outcomes, I don't believe the right response to accusations of softness is to create a tough façade. Neither do I believe that women leaders who are seen as harsh and demanding should instead become accommodating and sensitive. It makes much more sense to strive for a blend of the two qualities, weighted toward one's natural style. For instance, Susan Kropf was naturally tough because she demanded to know the details and drove hard to make sure policies were executed. At the same time, however, she was never brusque when she asked for information, and she exhibited a genuine concern for the people she interacted with. Susan Baer, former head of aviation for the Port Authority of New York and New Jersey, explained that she walked the tough/compassionate tightrope this way: "My leadership approach has always been to be decisive, because people want a decisive leader. I can be tough when I need to but I show compassion and caring as well."

There is no easy way out of this double-bind dilemma, but here are two things all women leaders should consider to manage it effectively:

- Recognize that the hard-soft issue isn't an either-or question. Women leaders don't have to choose between two opposing styles. It's a misconception that they can only be tough or only be soft. No boss—especially no male boss—should try and turn a woman leader into something she's not. Even the best-intentioned of male bosses shouldn't give feedback such as, "Unless you become as tough or tougher than any man on your team, you're not going to make it here," or, "You've got to stop being such a hard-ass and act more like a woman." Choosing to be one or the other guarantees inauthenticity.

- Favor the tilt (natural way of managing) that fits a given leadership style but develop the capacity to move to the other side when situations dictate. Some women are more naturally hard-edged and authoritative while others are more empathetic and inclusive. Women executives should know their tilt, and if they don't, organizations should provide feedback and coaching to help them discover it. They should also work to develop their nontilt side so that when a situation requires a different approach, they're ready.

LEVERAGING WOMEN'S INHERENT ADVANTAGES

In her book *How Women Are Transforming Leadership*, Mary Lou Dé-Costerd identified four traits that are natural to women and that help them succeed as organizational leaders.[11] Having interviewed or analyzed more than 100 of the world's most powerful women leaders, Dr. Décosterd has focused on characteristics that strike me as deeper and more relevant to leadership than the usual suspects (i.e., a woman's skill at communication). As a colleague of Dr. Décosterd, I've used these traits in my coaching practice and found them to be extraordinarily helpful to women leaders. Let's look at each of the four traits and how they can be used effectively in organizations:

- *Intuitive orientation*—This means the ability to see patterns, themes, and trends by envisioning future possibilities. Intuition isn't some magic, extrasensory ability women possess so much as the natural result of being alert, observant, and a good listener. Andrea was highly intuitive; she seemed to be one step ahead of everyone else as she reshaped Avon during her first six years on the job. Indra Nooyi, the CEO of PepsiCo, is another leader who capitalizes on her intuitive orientation: "I do believe that being a woman has helped me develop a unique adaptive approach to leadership that is critical in today's world of rapid change . . . leadership with open eyes, open ears, an open mind and an open heart."[12] Like Nooyi, women leaders need to take advantage of their inherent ability to be open-minded and observant—this ability activates intuition. Men may be more natural fact-based decision-makers, but women can often see emerging trends and ideas before anyone else.

- *Directive force*—Both men and women possess variations of this trait, which involves a singular focus in the pursuit of an objective. Men's directive force is usually individual, however, while women exercise a collective approach. Oprah Winfrey is a well-known example of a woman who brings various people together in a purposeful, driven manner to achieve goals. At Avon, Susan Kropf and Liz Smith both possessed directive force. Although the jury's still out on the success of Yahoo's CEO, Marissa Mayer, she clearly exemplifies the directive style. She was hired to turn around Yahoo and has been singular in her focus. She banned telecommuting so that the "coasters" would leave and the culture could be rebuilt through face-to-face conversations. Creating and using networks to achieve significant objectives is one way women can take advantage of this natural, directive force capability. Creating alliances, partnerships, and other collaborative groups is something that women often do extremely well and therefore should do more of.

- *Empowering intent*—This trait involves fostering responsibility in others. It sounds easy to do but can be challenging, especially for leaders who are powerful, directive, and controlling. To confer this sense of responsibility, women leaders don't simply tell people they're responsible for solving a problem or for carrying out a task but communicate their faith in them and offer them an eager ear and guidance without providing them with the answers. Brenda Barnes, former CEO of Sara Lee, was terrific at empowering others and responded to a question about how she got 50,000 people galvanized for the organization's turnaround and restructuring by saying, "We changed from 'Let me tell you the answer' to 'What do you think we ought to do?' Did we make them feel like they were worthwhile or did we make them feel like they weren't at all?"[13]

Susan Baer, when she was the first woman manager of the Lincoln Tunnel, inherited an organization that was run in a paramilitary style. Susan, though, recognized that she was unable to be an autocratic leader. Instead, she relied on her natural leadership style, which was maternal. She knew and cared about her people, treated them with respect, and gave them a great deal of responsibility. In the 1980s, Hurricane Gloria was bearing down on New York City and one of Susan's managers said, "We were racing through the Lincoln Tunnel facility to batten down the hatches for the impending hurricane. I said to Paul [a colleague], 'If you and I were owners of this tunnel, we would not be doing as good a job as we are because we're doing this for Sue.'"

Empowering, then, is communicating a sense of trust in others to do the job. That is much different than giving people responsibility. Susan Baer's employees wanted to do their jobs well to vindicate her trust in them. Creating a sense of confidence in others that they can perform a task well and on their own is what every woman leader should strive for.

- *Assimilative nature*—This may be the most nuanced of the four traits, in that being assimilative involves a variety of behaviors—bringing people and constructs together, listening deeply, being tolerant of differences, deepening dialogues by focusing on the most difficult parts of conversations. The Xerox Board chose Anne Mulcahy to be CEO precisely because she was an assimilator. As the company veered close to bankruptcy, the board must have been tempted to look for an outsider who could infuse the company with new ideas. Instead, they chose an insider who could bring people together—a wise decision, as it turned out. As Ursula Burns said of her former boss, "Her strength was aligning people, bringing them together to work toward a common goal."[14]

In increasingly diverse, global companies, a woman's ability to assimilate is more valuable than ever before. Unfortunately, because of the nuanced nature of this trait, organizations often don't reward its leaders for exhibiting it. Nonetheless, companies should recognize its value and encourage leaders to be more assimilative in a variety of situations. Leaders with the most diverse teams, that have wide-ranging discussions, and create a broad range of ideas and programs should be singled out for praise.

Finally, Décosterd makes the point that each of these traits are created equal. One isn't better than another; women shouldn't see assimilative nature as better than empowering intent, for instance. They also shouldn't strive for a purely assimilative or empowering style. All four traits are available to many female leaders, but the key is to be conscious of them and attempt to integrate them into their natural leadership styles.

TEN

TRAPS

Avoidance and Extrication Strategies

ULTIMATELY, ANDREA JUNG'S STORY IS A CAUTIONARY TALE FOR LEADERS. IF ANYONE seemed immune to failure, it was Andrea. She had so many strengths as a CEO and accomplished so much during the first half of her time at Avon that it was hard to imagine she would not lead Avon to greater glory.

Senior leaders must be strong and confident by definition, so they sometimes fail to see how vulnerable they and their organizations are. Consciously, they know that during times of instability and upheaval, they can be tripped up by a sudden economic shift, a new global competitor that appears seemingly out of nowhere, a huge new market that they've overlooked, an environmental disaster they haven't prepared for, or a technological breakthrough they haven't foreseen. Given the volatility we face today and in the future, these events aren't going away.

But they may not be as conscious of less obvious traps—anything from their own training to hidden weaknesses to the overwhelming nature of their jobs. My goal here is to provide organizations with a sense of the nine traps that catch many leaders unaware so they can avoid or solve them.

Andrea, like most CEOs, encountered these traps and dealt with some better than others. I interviewed a number of Andrea's colleagues at Avon and asked them to describe these traps, and I was surprised to hear significant differences of opinion as to the causes of Andrea's missteps. It occurred to me that sometimes, if we aren't aware of the real traps beneath the surface, we may seize on simple, but inaccurate, explanations.

Therefore, before identifying the nine traps that catch leaders, I'll provide a brief synopsis of how people responded when I asked them to tell me what they thought caused Andrea's and Avon's downfall.

TRAPS ARE IN THE EYE OF THE BEHOLDER

From some of the press reports, one might believe that Andrea failed because she ignored, or at least didn't pay enough attention to, the alleged unethical practices taking place in China. Yet what was the *real* trap here? Was it an unwillingness to confront her key people? Was it wishful thinking (that the problem would somehow go away on its own)? Was it a lack of strong support and oversight from the board? Was it a lack of knowledge about the situation? Was it a failure to install the proper controls? Was it the lack of discipline and rigor of the organization culture? People suggested all these possibilities and more.

Another interviewee suggested that Andrea and Avon fell because of bad luck. In a relatively short period of time, they were beset by the China bribery scandal that then expanded into other markets, the IT debacle in Brazil, the sudden spike in silver prices which weakened the financial impact of the Silpada acquisition, inventory management difficulties, and the downward spiral of Avon's US business. So who is responsible when bad things happen to good CEOs? It can be argued that bad things happen to all CEOs, and that the great ones anticipate these negative events, have early warning signs that alert them to potential disasters or allow them to respond in ways that minimize the damage. So did Andrea fall into the trap of not responding effectively to these negative events; did her pleaser personality prevent her from confronting certain people and taking tough stances?

Or was the trap fallen into by the board, rather than Andrea? Some people argued that the board may have been lulled into a false sense of security by Andrea's aura. They may have fallen into the trap of believing in the infallibility of their leader and may have failed to challenge the state of the business with a healthy dose of skepticism. They also didn't insist that Andrea develop a successor for COO—someone like Susan Kropf who possessed deep operational expertise. Some people said that Andrea failed because she stayed too long—she didn't have that internal career clock in her head that told her it was time to leave. Others suggested that Andrea and Avon were victims of the company's direct-selling model—it ceased to be as effective in the United States once the Internet became a widespread marketing tool. Critics also charged that the company did not take advantage of the Internet or social media early enough to drive sales and branding.

I could name 100 other possible traps and mistakes, but you get the idea. I've chosen nine that strike me as relevant to all leaders, across industries, and go deeper than "bad luck" or "lack of expertise." These nine often exist just outside a leader's consciousness. By writing about them here and explaining how to deal with them, I hope to raise everyone's awareness.

TRAP I: DISCOVERY VERSUS DELIVERY

In Chapter 7, I noted that leaders tend to tilt toward either the visionary, strategic side or the operation and execution side. In some instances, leaders are unaware of this tilt, deny it, or recognize it but fail to seek assistance in areas where they aren't naturally inclined or talented. After Susan left, Andrea believed that she still had strong operations people she could depend on. Andrea was a trusting leader, and for this reason, she assumed that they were taking care of the parts of the business that she wasn't good at or interested in. This assumption turned out to be a fatal mistake, especially at a time when the business desperately needed control and accountability.

Jeffery Dyer, Hal Gregersen, and Clay Christensen, researchers and practitioners and authors of the book *The Innovator's DNA: Mastering the Five Skills of Disruptive Innovators,* have coined terms that are better than mine at describing the visionary versus execution style.[1] They refer to "discovery-driven" and "delivery-driven." An example of the former is Steve Jobs; an example of the latter is Jack Welch. According to their research, discoverers are questioners, observers, and experimenters; deliverers are analyzers, planners, and detail-oriented.

As you might expect, Dyer, Gregersen, and Christensen's research suggests that the majority of CEOs of entrepreneurial-based companies are discovery-driven rather than delivery-driven but that these leaders can still be successful if they recognize their style and either worked to develop their own delivery capacities or brought in others to handle this second side of the business—think Steve Jobs bringing in Tim Cook. In addition, at times you want leaders who are more discovery-driven or more delivery-driven, depending on what challenges the organization is facing. For instance, if the company is focused on innovation, then discovery is key.

Most of the time, though, a balance is best. One way or another, leaders need to assess themselves (or even better, have others they trust and respect help with that assessment) and figure out where the unbalance is and how to fix it. If they fail to do so, they fall into a trap, the negative effects of which may take time to surface, but when they do, they can be devastating to organizations. In Avon's case, their inability to deliver (e.g., correct orders to the representatives, up-to-date IT systems, etc.) hurt them in the long run; they couldn't put controls and processes in place that were absolutely necessary for a global operation.

To avoid this trap, here are two sets of balancing actions to consider.

Delivery Strengthening Tactics

- Implement project management systems.
- Develop regular monitoring systems to assess progress. Sam Walton established Saturday morning meetings for store managers to discuss sales and ways to increase them.
- Designate an enforcer who has the skills to turn ideas into actions.
- Create analytic tools to facilitate data collection and interpretation.
- Keep scorecards to track progress on an ongoing basis.

Discovery Strengthening Tactics

- Benchmark companies outside of your industry.
- Go to conferences or forums outside of the norm for your company or industry to meet different people and gain exposure to fresh thinking.
- Analyze your network for diversity of experience, as well as diversity of thought. Seek new members if you find that network members are homogeneous.
- Try reverse mentorship (i.e., baby boomers getting mentored by a millennial).
- Go on field trips with your team to observe customers. This advice holds true even for leaders who don't have direct customer responsibilities, since every leader should possess customer insights and translate them into their areas of responsibility.

TRAP 2: TOO MANY DISTRACTIONS

CEOs and other top executives are besieged with requests for attendance and attention. The schedules of many CEOs are booked solid, not just during the workday, but nights and weekends as well. More than ever, they are inundated with both work-related events and tasks and external invitations—to participate in philanthropic groups, to serve on boards, to collaborate on industry-wide task forces. There is global travel, social media upkeep, and plenty more. Everything seems important—and to some degree, everything is—so leaders may fail to focus on what's most important.

The trap of doing too much without doing what's crucial is one that it seemed Andrea fell into. In addition to her external board commitments (GE and Apple), over the last two years of her tenure, it seemed as though everything seemed to go wrong for Andrea at the same time and that there were a multitude of programs and initiatives to reenergize, and fundamentals to fix. In the end, there's only so much any leader can give, and Andrea had more than a full plate with two separate governmental investigations going on, the loss of key talent, and an economic downturn. Admittedly, there's not a lot Andrea or any CEO can do about some of these distractions, but limiting the number of programs and commitments made and the time spent on noncore business activities is a good first step. Here are some other actions that I've found help leaders avoid this trap:

- Establish a laser-like focus. Lou Gerstner was said to be able to concentrate on essential tasks and had the discipline to see them through no matter what else was going on around him. Though it's difficult to eliminate all the distractions, it is possible to ignore them for a period of time to focus on a matter that requires a leader's undivided attention. This is as opposed to the unfocused or scattered leader who jumps from topic to topic in a frenzy and is never able to sit still long enough to give the essential subjects the time they deserve.
- Use the calendar review method. When I coach leaders, I sometimes ask them to review their calendars for the last year and ask them how their various activities match up with the

company's critical business objectives. I don't judge anything we find on the calendar, since people reflexively judge themselves. They are able to see perfectly well that they spent half of March on meaningless lunches, meetings that others could have attended, items that could have been delegated, and trade show events and that they could have used that time to focus on a big problem confronting the business, interacting with customers, identifying future trends that could impact the business, or coaching their people.

- Ask yourself a series of tough questions about how you're spending your time. These questions include the following: What key business decisions or issues have you been neglecting? Why have you been neglecting them? Is it that you lack the time to concentrate on them? Is it that you prefer the glamour and fun of other activities to hard choices involving subjects that you're not an expert at? Are you willing to make a commitment to shut yourself off from other responsibilities to deal with mission-critical issues? Are you willing to ask others (who have more expertise in these areas than you do) for help to push aside the distractions?

TRAP 3: FUNCTIONAL FAVORITISM

Every organization favors certain functions and work styles over others. At Avon, sales and marketing ruled the roost, and the culture was relationship-driven. It was not detail-oriented, process-dependent, or controls-focused. There's nothing wrong with a company having a natural leaning toward a certain function or style of operating, but there is something wrong when they can't deviate from that leaning even when circumstances dictate they should. Agility is crucial in this day and age, and when an innovative, marketing-oriented culture like Avon's has trouble shifting to more operations and detail-oriented mode as the business changes, then the company is caught in a favoritism trap.

Large organizations in the pharmaceutical industry, for instance, are conscious of the need to avoid favoritism and balance two opposing functions—the creative functions such as marketing and R&D and the process functions such as manufacturing and regulatory. While a given pharmaceutical company may lean more in one direction than another, it usually recognizes that it can't compete successfully if it stubbornly adheres to one approach while subordinating the other. To avoid this trap, organizations need to find the right balance point based on the current issues they are facing and the expertise that's needed. More specifically, here are a few ways to find this balance point:

- Manage the tensions between the two opposing camps. Marketing, for instance, always feels that regulatory is nitpicking, while regulatory believes that marketing is ignoring the rules, to the company's peril. If these tensions are allowed to run rampant, it not only creates discord within the organization but also results in politicking by each faction and a win-lose mentality. Savvy leaders acknowledge and celebrate the natural tensions. Apple, for instance, has done a great job of this. In some ways, the real lesson here is to value both the creative tasks of a business and the more mundane, but no less essential, execution requirements. After all, it takes both to make a successful, functional product. A company that places a high priority on having the best-designed products or the most compelling advertising and a low priority on delivering products to meet demand can survive for a while on its creativity, but it will ultimately lose.
- Make sure the senior team makes situational, rather than functionally biased, choices. As I stated earlier, people take their cues from the CEO's behaviors. If the CEO seems to favor decisions by the numbers, everyone will be numbers-obsessed. The behavior to model is situational—be sufficiently agile to

choose sides based on what's needed at the time and not based on your functional path and preferences.

TRAP 4: OVERSPECIALIZATION

In some organizations, the top leaders are experts, often brilliant ones. They excel in one area—finance, operations, marketing, engineering—and their talent has helped them achieve a lot for the company and for themselves. They are stars, albeit ones blazing a narrow path. Andrea, of course, was brilliant at marketing (plus, she had charisma to burn), and this talent took her to the top quickly. As I've noted, however, her lack of experience in operations hurt her. While many studies have been done about what's the best degree and background for an effective CEO, few definitive conclusions have been reached.

Based on my own experiences and research, however, it strikes me that the broader the background of a leader, the more successful he or she will be. Narrowly trained leaders tend to hit a wall when the organization needs knowledge or experience they lack. Even if they are narrower in skills, however, good CEOs should be aware of this "deficit" and hire people who possess the competencies they lack. I would argue however, given the global complexity of running large organizations today, the best background for a CEO would include some level of supply chain expertise. In fact, the article "CEOs with a Functional Background in Operations: Reviewing Their Performance and Prevalence in the Top Post" posits that because the supply chain cuts across functions, leaders who come from that background are better able to break down functional silos and coordinate across functional operations.[2]

At Avon, Andrea was the ideal CEO when the company needed her branding skill and charisma. When it needed someone who was great at processes and details, though, the company suffered. Too often, money went to R&D or advertising that should have been funneled into IT or elsewhere. This wasn't just because of Andrea. Directly and indirectly, organizations tend to hire people who mirror the talents and sensibilities of their CEOs. When Avon's Brazil operation suffered losses because they had difficultly implementing the government's mandated e-invoicing systems, it was an indirect result of a talent planning and promotion process that favored Andrea-like competencies. One global executive told me, "The General Manager [in Brazil] was more focused on the commercial side of the business. He was not an Ops guy." He added that Brazil's IT person also didn't like confrontation (like Andrea) and wasn't good at bringing the general manager bad news or dealing with problems directly and decisively.

It's impossible to staff all top leadership positions with individuals who have diverse backgrounds and multiple competencies, but the trap of overspecialization can be avoided in other ways, including:

- Be willing to select against the expected specialty. Tech companies, for instance, have plenty of executives who possess significant technological skills. What they may have in short supply are leaders with other competencies. Lou Gerstner, when he was chosen to head IBM, was a nontech leader who had turnaround skills—this was exactly what IBM needed at this point in their evolutionary cycle. Similarly, former Xerox CEO Anne Mulcahy called herself the accidental CEO, because she didn't fit the CEO profile—she lacked operations experience and was a long-tenured staffer—but she became the agent of change that the company required. Certainly there is value in having a leader who knows a given business thoroughly, but there is also value in thinking counterintuitively. The trap of overspecialization is also the trap of homogeneity—organizations sometimes have leaders who possess leadership styles, thinking, and expertise that aren't typical for these organizations.
- Set a two-function minimum for top position selection. Cross-functional training assignments are great, but what's even better for escaping the overspecialization trap is solid, sustained work

experience in more than one function. A diverse group of cross-functional experiences is terrific preparation for understanding how all the organizational pieces fit together. More than ever before, running a global company involves a series of complexities. To deal with these complicated and confusing issues, a deep understanding of different functions—marketing and production, for instance—and how they interrelate is crucial. This prevents CEOs from running a multifunction organization from a single-function mindset.

• Value eclectic business and educational experiences. Admittedly, it may depend on the individual company and their strategy, but if I were on a board selection committee searching for a new CEO for my company, some of my criteria would include a work assignment of six months to two years spent in another country; significant financial experience and knowledge from advanced degrees in finance to work on the financial side of the business or profit and loss responsibility (to facilitate dealing with complex global financial practices); a track record of working on and managing cross-functional teams effectively; and at least one job that required customer interaction. I'd also value candidates who took a sabbatical to explore an interest, who enjoy traveling around the world, who went back to school to study a subject that they're passionate about, who attend seminars and workshops in areas outside of their areas of expertise. Well-rounded leaders don't get caught in the overspecialization trap.

• Find leaders who are active learners. CEOs who avoid the trap of overspecialization often make efforts—sometimes extraordinary ones—to develop a great breadth and depth of knowledge about running the business. When Anne Mulcahy first took over as CEO of a near-bankrupt Xerox, she knew that having a command of the financials would be critical so she asked the staff in the treasurer's group to tutor her before

critical meetings, especially ones with bankers.[3] Not every
CEO is comfortable seeking knowledge outside of their area of
expertise or their functional specialty. They may be much more
comfortable delegating these tasks to others with appropriate
expertise and possess neither the patience nor the initiative to
learn generally. Some CEOs, though, make it their business
to know what needs to be known and seek to gain at least a
rudimentary knowledge of these subjects.

TRAP 5: TYPECASTING

Many leaders are capable of growth and change yet choose to stick
to what they know. Everyone tells them that they're great marketers
or operations people or financial geniuses, and they believe this is all
that they can and should be. Yet these self-imposed limits are a trap. As
organizations change, leaders need to change with them or they'll be
leading from positions of weakness. Andrea heeded consultant Ram
Charan's advice to fire and rehire herself, moving from a marketer to a
globalizer and cost cutter. Practically speaking, she went from a CEO
who relied on innovation and pizzazz to launch new, image-conscious
businesses to a turnaround-focused, new-process implementer. Andrea
essentially refused to be who everyone said she was.

Most leaders today will be working in businesses that change significantly from the time they're hired to only a few years in. I coached
Jean, a general manager, who was known and admired for her conservative, financial-savvy approach to the business—an approach that was
valued when she first joined the company and helped right the ship.
Over time, though, Jean was perceived to be out of touch with emerging trends and unwilling to embrace innovation or risk. To escape the
trap of typecasting, Jean made a lateral move to a group that incubated
new businesses that might one day fit into the company's core business.
As a result, Jean gained valuable experience and expertise working with
cutting-edge companies. More to the point, it gave her a way to lead

differently—she gained a track record and reputation as a more daring, in-touch executive.

To escape this trap, take this bold step:

- Rebrand yourself. This doesn't mean just talking a new game—proclaiming that you're now a bottom-line guy when you used to be a roll-the-dice player—but crafting a new substance to back the style. To a certain extent, you may be limited by your abilities and time; you're not going to segue from 20 years as a sales pro to a tech expert or global mastermind overnight. But rebranding is possible for everyone as long as you're realistic about moving from point A to point B. To that end, understand how you're currently perceived as a leader versus how you want to be perceived, given the organization's evolution and new requirements. Identify the work experiences, educational options, and other factors that can help you bridge the gap. As you rebrand yourself, you may discover that it's not just you but your entire management team that has to learn and grow in order to be effective. In some instances, a narrow focus is not just a flaw of one leader but of the entire team, and that's when rebranding becomes a group project.

TRAP 6: NOT HEARING THE BAD NEWS

Most CEOs and other top executives say that they want to hear the unvarnished truth, and most mean it. But it's the rare subordinate who actually follows this directive. This trap is insidious because while leaders think they're getting the bad news as well as the good, their people are actually filtering what they hear. Andrea made it a point to solicit people's views and requested that people be honest with her. More than most leaders, she created an open environment that encouraged straight talk, with no risk of retribution. Shortly after becoming CEO, she set up the CEO Advisory Council, which was composed of high-potential leaders from around the world. The purpose of the Council was to provide Andrea with unfiltered feedback about any and every issue.

Still, people withheld information and opinions, especially after Andrea had been CEO for a few years. Andrea inspired intense loyalty, and while this loyalty had a number of benefits, it also prevented people from disappointing her. They would rationalize that they could handle a situation on their own and that she didn't need to be bothered. In her last few years on the job, when things were going wrong left and right, this loyalty-inspired filtering of news was particularly problematic, as she was repeatedly blindsided by a problem that would have been much easier to solve in its early stages.

Some CEOs, of course, aren't like Andrea and give the impression they may kill the messenger, whether this is true or not. So bearers of bad tidings learn to sugarcoat negative news out of fear of being punished.

There's also the issue of long-tenured leaders. I've found that not only Andrea but other leaders are extraordinarily open to all ideas and information when they first take on their job; they're hungry to learn. Over time, however, they feel confident that they know what's going on, become less active in seeking out all types of people and information, and eventually rely on a narrow group of people for feedback. This limiting of sources can shield them from bad news, especially if it's occurring outside the organization. In many cases, they aren't aware of negative trends and events until it's too late.

Thus, getting the bad news is more difficult than it might appear. To remedy this situation, try the following:

- Don't be a scary boss. Again, this probably isn't an intentional perception, but people often overreact to what senior leaders say and do. I coached a very senior leader who kept a punching bag in his office. Rather than assure employees that at least he'd take out his anger on an inanimate object, they felt they could very well be that punching bag if they said the wrong thing. So the key here is for leaders to keep their tempers in check and react in a calm and considered way, no matter how upset they might be by what they're hearing. This is especially true for leaders with a volatile derailer. I worked with a not-for-profit executive who was so passionate about his work that when someone disagreed with him, he reacted with righteous indignation. The passion and volume of his response discouraged people from saying anything that might cause him to respond with unbridled fury. This executive's conscious goal wasn't to discourage dissent and upsetting, negative news, but nevertheless, it had this effect.

- Determine if you're unconsciously blocking bad news (and ask for feedback from others that you know may not always be willing to give you the straight story). Does it seem as if your people are working overtime not to disappoint you? Are you perceived as intimidating? Do you tend to dominate conversations? Do you have a reputation for being the smartest person in the room (Ivy League grad, high IQ, fast track jobs, etc.)? People who answer yes to some or all of these questions may unintentionally stop others from telling them bad news. Do you have enough truth tellers around you?

- Make an effort to seek information outside of the regular channels. Another way of putting this: Don't rely exclusively on your inner circle for facts and opinions. Susan Kropf, as noted earlier, had such terrific, two-way lines of communication that no matter what issue arose, she always knew who to call within Avon and was certain to get unfiltered information. Xerox's former CEO Anne Mulcahy said, "Keeping in touch with and having those relationships to the people on the ground is so valuable, in terms of having knowledge that allows you to provide direction to run the company."[4] Leaders who actively seek a diversity of viewpoints and data and who form wide-ranging networks to get this information are the ones who rarely fall into the bad news trap.

- Challenge your view of reality. Every leader finds herself confronted with information at some point that suggests her long-held belief or way of doing business may be wrong. At first, this can seem the worst kind of news, and some people react by going into denial. Escape this trap by being open to opposing (to your own) ideas and information. Monitor the little voice in your head that is trying to fit everything into your view of reality and recognize that this voice may be leading you astray.

TRAP 7: RESPONDING TO MESSAGES FROM HOME UNCONSCIOUSLY

By messages from home, I'm referring to the lessons we were taught growing up and that remain influential on our behaviors as adults. I'm not going to rehash all the work done on the relationship between personality and leadership here except to reference a leadership development program I attended years ago at the Center for Creative Leadership (CCL) conducted by former CCL senior fellow Kerry Bunker. He explained how, growing up, we heard certain messages repeatedly from our family, and some of them helped us adopt positive behaviors while others were negative and became problems in the workplace. A simple example is the kid who heard the message, "A penny saved is a penny earned," and grew up to be a manager who refused to give decent raises and bonuses and lost some of his best people because of his frugality. One message I received from my father growing up was, "Think before you act." As I result, I used to create what I felt were perfect presentations and programs—I put a tremendous amount of thought into them before sharing them with my staff. Consequently, when anyone responded to these "perfect" presentations with anything less than unadulterated praise, I became defensive (which I became aware of through 360-degree feedback). I realized that I was trying too hard for perfection, both making me defensive when I received criticism and not leaving any room for a collaborative process that could make the work

I had done better. Only when I became conscious of my message from home could I adapt my behaviors—I learned to present programs that weren't as polished and to become more receptive to feedback.

Of course, messages from home can be positive as well as negative—there is certainly value in thinking before acting in certain situations. But when leaders aren't conscious of these messages, then they are much more likely to be influenced by their negative aspects.

Andrea talked a great deal about the messages she received growing up, and they included:

- Don't be boastful or arrogant.
- Be courteous, sensitive to others, and transform your anger into helpful, positive emotions.
- This family never quits; it perseveres.[5]

It would have been better for Andrea and Avon if she had left a few years before she did. But her message from home was so powerful—this family never quits—that departing with the company in flux would have been against her nature.

To escape this trap, the key is awareness. While leaders need to be aware of their childhood messages—and Andrea certainly recognized her own—they also must understand how these messages affect what they say and do within their organizations. They must question regularly if they are inclined to make a choice because it's the right one or because it would have gained approval from parents or other role models. It sounds simple, but in the crush of today's competitive business landscape, leaders often fail to heed my childhood message—they act without thinking or at least don't think about those messages that have been hard-wired into them.

TRAP 8: UNBRIDLED OPTIMISM

My colleagues Bruce Avolio and Fred Luthans have found a positive correlation between increased business performance and job satisfaction and what they refer to as psychological capital—a mix of optimism, resilience, confidence, and hope.[6] So optimism is good, and there's no question that Andrea could not have led Avon successfully during her first five years at the helm without it.

At a certain point, however, leaders cross the line and instead of possessing the psychological capital of which Avolio and Luthans refer to, they are mired in unrealistic optimism, a dangerous trap. Instead of making significant changes, organizations caught in this trap accept the status quo.

Avon's board was overly optimistic about Andrea's chances of turning around the company during the last few years when she was CEO. They were influenced by her halo, which still had a great deal of wattage. They had seen how she had helped produce double-digit growth during her first five years on the job. And they had watched her orchestrate one major turnaround already, so it seemed that she might be able to do it again. But if they had analyzed the situation objectively, they would have recognized that it was tough sledding ahead and that they might have needed a CEO with different expertise than Andrea possessed to help them transition to a new and improved Avon.

To avoid the trap of unbridled optimism, try the following:

- Make a conscious effort to identify the negative side of an optimistic perspective. I'm not suggesting adopting a negative attitude but rather finding a balance point between optimism and realism. No matter how optimistic a leader or a team is about a situation, they should always ask, "What can go wrong?" and "Is our enthusiasm for the project blinding us to potential obstacles?" Creating a list of pros and cons is the most basic way of finding a balance point, but leaders should also work both sides of their brain—to come at an issue with great enthusiasm and optimism but also with a devil's advocate-like skepticism.

TRAP 9: DERAILERS

I've talked about this issue before, but I want to include it as this chapter's final trap because it's the one that gets most leaders. Derailers are subtle, and they often are seen as strengths rather than weaknesses because a derailer is the flip side of a leadership strength, for example, the highly confident, decisive individual that without even knowing it, can cross the line and be perceived as arrogant. As a result, derailers can afflict leaders before they know what hit them.

I won't provide a lengthy discussion about derailers themselves (for a more in-depth look, read *Why CEO's Fail*, by David Dotlich and Peter Cairo, or take a look at the Hogan Assessment System, and more specifically the Hogan Development Survey, the results of which are often referred to more colloquially as derailers).[7] What I'd like to do, though, is review some of Andrea's derailers and how they impacted her as a leader and then suggest what can be done to manage derailers and minimize harm.

Andrea was a Pleaser in derailer terms. According to Dotlich and Cairo, these individuals are skilled at "anticipating and meeting expectations . . . are highly astute at figuring out what other people want. They're not spineless followers: they possess a keen political sense and have an uncanny knack of delivering the right resources, information and ideas to the right people at the right time."[8] Andrea could do all this and more. Collaboration and consensus-building as well as marketing all abilities that come naturally to the Pleaser. Under stress, however, the negative side of the Pleaser may emerge. These were the times when Andrea would struggle to make tough calls, act as if leadership were a popularity contest, and reverse a decision if she thought people were unhappy with a choice she had made.

Andrea also was Aloof. This may seem odd, as she was often described as charming, and people felt extraordinarily loyal to and protective of her. But she was never particularly close with most of her employees (the Aloof type may be close with a select few—the inner circle), at least on a personal level. On the positive side, Aloof leaders are often smart, analytical, and highly professional. On the negative side, though, their inability to connect with a diverse and large number of individuals limits their networks. In times of crisis, especially, they retreat into their own heads or depend on a trusted few advisors. Consequently, they don't receive a true diversity of opinion and ideas, thus limiting their course of action. President Obama, like Andrea, fits this type; the opposite would be former president Bill Clinton.

How can CEOs and other senior leaders manage their derailers and prevent themselves from being trapped by their types? Here are some approaches that I've found to be effective:

- Identify derailers. Understand what the common derailers are and the ones that apply to a given leader. Recognize, too, that one side of the derailer is a strength but that too much of it can limit effectiveness—confidence is good, but too much confidence becomes arrogance. Many times, the people who know leaders best—usually their families—know what these derailers are and have been managing around them for years.

- Understand the circumstances under which these derailers emerge—usually stressful circumstances. Ideally, leaders will learn to eliminate or minimize this stress and its cause. If this is not possible, then they must improve their ability to recognize when they are under great stress and develop alternative behaviors to cope with it productively. Andrea practiced delivering the tough messages and developing the confidence to deal with the worst-case scenarios—highly stressful events for her.

- Use the mindset/behavior model. When coaching leaders who are trying to manage their derailers, I have them first identify how their mindset has to change and then how their behavior has to change. This may seem like semantics, but breaking the process into two steps is a good way to deal with derailers. For instance, I had a client whose mindset was often skeptical and who responded to this mindset by acting reserved (becoming silent or close to silent). When one of his people made a proposal that he was skeptical about, he'd respond with stony silence—a response that alienated his direct reports and made them reluctant to propose anything that they thought might make their boss mute. My client focused on his mindset first, changing the little voice in his head that responded with skepticism when people would make proposals. Instead of that voice telling him, "He's just saying that because he thinks you want to hear it," he altered the voice so that he heard, "Give him a chance; he has expertise in this area." Then, instead of reflexively becoming silent (his typical behavior), he would force himself to ask the presenter at least two questions. In this way, he stopped automatically lapsing into his skeptical/reserved mode.

These tactics help raise self-awareness about derailers, and this awareness may be all that's needed to prevent a derailer's negative effects, especially during times of stress when we tend to respond reflexively rather than thoughtfully.

As you can see, Avon and Andrea were skilled at avoiding some of these traps while they struggled to extricate themselves from others. Awareness of the nine traps combined with use of the tactics listed in each trap discussion will help organizations sidestep at least some of the common snares that would otherwise cause them serious problems. As important as the Avon/Andrea story is in alerting companies to these traps, it also provides a to-do list for the coming years.

ELEVEN

THE LEADERSHIP TO-DO LIST

ONE OF THE PREMISES OF THIS BOOK IS THAT ANDREA JUNG'S 13 YEARS AT AVON OFFER AN extraordinary opportunity to learn valuable leadership lessons. Reading the story of Andrea's triumphs and tribulations, you may have naturally applied those lessons to your own organization—at least I hope so. Here, I offer a final take-away, thoughts on what organizations can do now and in the years ahead to maximize the value of these lessons.

In composing this list, I tried to focus on the strategic imperatives we all wrestle with in a business environment of ever-increasing volatility and complexity. When facing the growth challenges and various crises that Avon's leadership faced, what should enterprises do?

Here are ten recommendations:

1. *Know the organization's place in its evolutionary cycle.* In Chapter 7, I listed five evolutionary phases—creativity, direction, delegation, coordination, and collaboration—and explained why companies must select leaders who fit the phase the organization happens to be in. This cycle has sped up in recent years and will move even faster in the future. Consider that not very long ago, no one had heard of Groupon, Tumblr, Pinterest, and many others. They went from the creativity phase to the collaboration phase with astonishing quickness. On top of that, reinvention

has become a corporate buzz word, and as mature enterprises reinvent themselves, they may cycle back and forth through various evolutionary stages. While leaders may know their current organizational goals and strategies, they need to remain open to new information as they shift from one phase to the next. Does their senior team possess the requisite knowledge and skills to manage this phase effectively? Is there awareness of each individual's strengths and weaknesses? Is the company disciplined in their approach to talent, making sure they measure existing competencies as they mature and evolve? If Avon had been able to answer these questions, Andrea might still be the lionized CEO of the company today.

2. *Approach CEO succession as if the organization's life depends on it.* Too often, boards view their succession responsibilities from the perspective of, "What will we do if the CEO gets hit by a bus?" That's a fair question, but it's only one of many. For instance, if the internal bench is limited, should we bring in external hires who can be groomed for this role? Are we monitoring the designated successor's development to ensure he or she is receiving optimal coaching, experiences, and so on? As much as boards may admire the current CEO, and good as that CEO may be, they need to be objective and diligent in their evaluations and succession planning. Boards often rely on processes to evaluate CEO leadership effectiveness, and they need to establish similar processes for succession-related tasks. In the past, this type of process was less important, both because CEOs tended to stay in place longer and because a less volatile environment required less shuffling of the deck. Today, it doesn't take much change for a CEO's skills to be less well-suited to the organization or for a successor to grow impatient and bolt to another organization.

3. *Manage paradoxes.* At Avon, paradoxes abounded: global versus local, short-term results versus long-term sustainability, centralized versus decentralized. At times, the company committed the

sin of trying to manage them through wild swings in business direction—one year they went all out to decentralize the system, the next they swung back to centralized control. Paradoxes proliferate during times of upheaval, uncertainty, and continuous change. Thus, we can expect more of them in the years ahead. To manage them effectively requires a willingness to accept the validity of two seemingly opposing positions. Rather than chose one or the other, organizations must develop the agility to accommodate both sides as legitimate and consider both in the decision-making process. Avon learned that it couldn't embrace one business construct (creating a globally consistent brand) and reject another (the idiosyncrasies and requirements of local markets), but it took a while before they learned to accommodate both.

4. *Find the right mix of disparate people, policies, and processes.* The ingredients for success are more complex than in the past. At Avon, we saw what happened when one ingredient was missing: when Susan Kropf retired, the absence of deep operations expertise created huge problems. Companies can't succeed in a highly competitive global marketplace with great strategies and mediocre execution. They can't succeed if they overlook the natural tensions between marketing and regulatory, for example, and if they fail to have people in place who can work effectively together despite these tensions. The right mix is different for every organization, but close attention to the ingredients is more important than ever.

5. *Identify the business you're in . . . and redefine that identity as necessary.* The ground is shifting under everyone's feet these days, and assuming you're still in the business you started in can be a mistake. At Avon, leadership was never clear on whether they were a beauty company or a direct-selling one. Initially, Andrea saw it as a beauty company, while others opted for direct selling. The problem, of course, is that rapid change renders formerly viable

definitions obsolete; the direct-selling model was quickly going the way of the Model T, at least in the United States. Even relatively young companies are being forced to redefine themselves, or at least rethink their core identities. When Sheryl Sandberg joined Facebook as COO, for instance, she didn't simply take the core company concept as a given but she spent a number of months with her staff discussing the business they were in and how to make it a profitable business. Through these discussions, she and her staff began to reframe business profitability in terms of advertising. The best CEOs today see themselves as chief communicators and cheerleaders, and in these roles, they broadcast what the company is all about and work to gain alignment around that identity.

6. *Be extraordinarily vigilant in at-risk global markets.* More and more Western-based companies are doing business in China, Russia, Brazil, Vietnam, India, Dubai, South Africa, and elsewhere. The rewards these markets offer can be offset by the risks—by scandals, political upheavals, and failed investments. Avon experienced the bribery scandal in China as well as technology snafus in Brazil, both of which hurt the company in different ways. Avon thought it was doing a good job in both markets, and in some ways they were, but they failed to realize that China was a time bomb because of the complex set of business practices that went on and that the company would be caught unaware in Brazil by government-mandated new technology. And it's not just Avon. The increasing aggressiveness of the US Department of Justice and the Securities Exchange Commission resulted in 91 US-based companies involved in ongoing investigations of violations of FCPA as of June 2013. Consider, too, the amount of money involved in these investigations. As of 2013, Avon spent $340 million on their investigation, and Walmart forecasted fees of more than $300 million related to their investigations of alleged bribery in Mexico in exchange for prime real estate locations for

their new stores. For these reasons, it behooves organizations to do ethics and FCPA training for people in these at-risk markets, to hire diverse, ethical leaders for these markets who understand the US laws and appreciate the nuances of doing business there and develop oversight processes for these markets and agree on internal investigatory protocols to follow if problems develop in these countries.

7. *Align the culture and the strategy.* Aligning culture and strategy may not always have been top-of-mind awareness for CEOs—if they were even aware of it at all. Andrea certainly was aware of this task, although she struggled at times to create this alignment initially. Perhaps she underestimated the power of the culture to undermine even the strongest strategy. Now and in the next five years, organizations are going to be embarking on new and sometimes controversial strategies in order to keep pace with a changing business environment. As these strategies are launched, clashes may occur with long-standing cultures, especially as many companies continue their globalization strategy. While there's no way to avoid these clashes, they can be managed, and the first steps in doing so involves understanding what that culture is all about, preserving what is crucial for the company and that engages the work force, and then evolving the culture in fresh and appropriate directions. The key, though, is never discussing strategy without factoring in its impact on the culture.

8. *Impose term limits.* While most research agrees that executives need to be in a job for two or three years to develop the knowledge that leads to success, little research exists on how long is too long to be in a job. Generally, seven to ten years seems to be the optimum length of time for CEOs to serve. After a few years of riding the learning curve that exists in every CEO position, they can operate with a high degree of effectiveness for perhaps five or six years. Then many CEOs settle into their roles and develop comfortable routines, losing some of that edge that they had early on.

They may no longer be the ideal leader for the company as the external environment changes and the company needs to change with it (as happened eventually with Andrea). While some CEOs may be capable of operating at a high degree of effectiveness for ten, twelve, or more years, most lack this capability. Given the need for many companies to reinvent themselves—a need that will only increase in the future—it seems as if term limits for CEOs would benefit the majority of organizations (not to mention preserving the CEO's legacy).

9. *Fight second-order gender bias.* Despite the significant progress that has been made toward gender equality in business, there's still more progress to be made. Second-order gender bias refers to subtle prejudice that emerges from organizational structures, practices, patterns of interactions, and so on. Avon, as the company for women, did a great job of avoiding any kind of gender bias during Andrea's time there. Unfortunately, other organizations don't always achieve this same standard. Though overt bias against women isn't common anymore, and there are an increasing number of female CEOs, there still are barriers that prevent some women from finding game-changer roles—positions that are critical for entry into the senior management ranks. They are denied these roles for a variety of reasons, that is, they require a great deal of time and commitment and the assumption is that women with kids won't be willing to handle it. Or it's assumed that women are too soft to handle the demands of these roles. Whatever the reason, the subtle bias that prevents entry to senior management hurts organizations. More than ever, companies need the most qualified people in leadership roles, and anything that prevents this from happening should be addressed and eliminated.

10. *Foster leadership self-awareness.* This means providing leaders with coaching and other tools that help them understand their strengths and weaknesses and how their behaviors affect others.

Andrea was more self-aware than many leaders, but I don't think she ever was fully aware of how her aura affected others. Just as she wanted to please others, others wanted to please her, and in some instances, that meant holding back bad news. She also seemed vulnerable at times, and while it's endearing that her direct reports wanted to protect her, this behavior may be counterproductive. Leaders need to receive the unvarnished truth from their people, and I'm not sure Andrea always received it. Self-awareness also means recognizing your derailers. When leaders know they're prone to actions such as being arrogant, focusing too much on pleasing others, or other unproductive behaviors, they and their organizations are less likely to be harmed by derailer-based reactions. Coaches, mentors, human resources professionals, and others can work with leaders on their derailers, and they should be encouraged to do so.

Most leaders possess lengthy to-do lists, and my objective here is not to create more burdensome tasks but to focus attention on crucial actions that may be overlooked or not even considered—actions that are especially imperative now and in the years ahead. These neglected actions emerge when you study one leader in one company in an in-depth manner—especially someone like Andrea Jung, whose greatness every leader should aspire to and whose flaws every leader should be wary of. Putting a leader under the microscope can reveal truths that might otherwise escape us. If this book reveals these truths, then we all owe a debt of gratitude to Andrea and Avon for what they have taught us.

NOTES

CHAPTER I

1. Video interview from Makers, July 31, 2012, www.makers.com/andrea-jung.
2. Ibid.
3. Andrea Jung speech, Tsinghua University, October 23, 2003.
4. Andrea Jung speech, Princeton Career Services, Imagine Speaker series, You-Tube, uploaded January 16, 2012.
5. Andrea Jung, GoldSea interview, http://goldsea.com/WW/Jungandrea/jung andrea.html.
6. Patricia Sellers, "Behind Every Successful Woman There Is . . . A Woman," *Fortune* Magazine, October 25,1999, 129.
7. Bill George, Diana Mayer, and Andrew N. "Andrea Jung: Empowering Avon Women (A)," Harvard Business School, Case 9–404–035, January 28, 2008.
8. Ibid.
9. Ibid.
10. Video interview, Makers, July 31, 2012.

CHAPTER 2

1. Video interview from Makers, July 31, 2012, www.makers.com/andrea-jung.
2. Bill George, Diana Mayer, and Andrew N., "Andrea Jung: Empowering Avon Women (A)," Harvard Business School, Case 9–404–035, January 28, 2008.
3. Ramin Setoodeh, "Calling Avon's Lady," *Newsweek*, December 26, 2004.
4. George, Mayer, and Andrew N., "Andrea Jung."
5. Rachel Beck, "Andrea Jung Gives Makeup Seller a Complete Makeover," *The Daily Courier*, January 26, 1999.
6. Sean Menegan, "Andrea Jung: Maintaining Spirit Among the Troops While Revamping Product Lines." *Brandweek*, October 7, 1996: 98–102.
7. David Dotlich, Peter Cairo, and Cade Cowan, *The Unfinished Leader: Balancing Contradictory Answers to Unsolvable Problems* (New York: Jossey-Bass, 2014).
8. Video interview, Makers, July 31, 2012.
9. George, Mayer, and Andrew N., "Andrea Jung."

CHAPTER 3

1. Video interview from Makers, July 31, 2012, www.makers.com/andrea-jung.

2. Laura Klepacki, *Avon: Building the World's Premier Company for Women* (Hoboken, NJ: John Wiley and Sons, 2005).

CHAPTER 4

1. Avon press release, July 10, 2001.
2. Laura Klepacki, *Avon: Building the World's Premier Company for Women* (Hoboken, NJ: John Wiley and Sons, 2005).
3. Ibid.

CHAPTER 5

1. Interview with Charlie Rose, YouTube, uploaded November 26, 2010.
2. Avon press release, October 20, 2008.

CHAPTER 6

1. Beth Kowitt, "The Rise and Fall of a Beauty Icon," *Fortune*, April 11, 2012.
2. Avon press release, December 13, 2011.
3. Hannah Karp and Joann S. Lublin, "Former CEOs Criticize Avon," *Wall Street Journal*, December 22, 2011.
4. Emily Glazer, "Avon Chairman, Andrea Jung to Resign; Fred Hassan to Take Over," *Wall Street Journal*, October 5, 2012.
5. Kowitt, "Rise and Fall of a Beauty Icon."

CHAPTER 7

1. Larry Greiner, "Evolution and Revolution as Organizations Grow," *in Developing Managerial Skills in Organizational Behavior: Exercises, Cases, and Readings* by L. Mainiero and C. Tromley, 2nd ed. (Englewood Cliffs, NJ: Prentice Hall, 1994), 00322–29.
2. Nathan Bennett and Stephen A. Miles, *Riding Shotgun: The Role of the COO* (Stanford, CA: Stanford University Press, 2006).
3. Ken Auletta, "A Woman's Place," *New Yorker*, July 11, 2011.
4. George Anders, "The Reluctant Savior of Hewlett-Packard," *Forbes*, June 10, 2013, 76.
5. Ibid.
6. Ankur Agrawal, John Goldie, and Bill Hoyett, "Today's CFO: Which Profile Best Suits Your Company?" *McKinsey & Company: Insights and Publications*, January 2013.

CHAPTER 8

1. Louis V. Gerstner, *Who Says Elephants Can't Dance?* (New York: HarperCollins, 2002), 182.
2. Bethany McLean and Peter Elkind, *The Smartest Guys in the Room: The Amazing Rise and Scandalous Fall of Enron* (New York: Penguin, 2003).
3. Gerstner, *Who Says Elephants Can't Dance?* 23.
4. Ibid., 189.
5. Kodak: Interview with Dr. George Fisher, Video. By Giovanni Gavetti, Harvard Business School. October 1, 2005.

CHAPTER 9

1. Rosabeth Moss Kanter, *Men and Women of the Corporation* (New York, N.Y: Basic Books, 1977).
2. Transcript of Andrea Jung speech, "Avon's Andrea Jung: You Will Stand on my Shoulders," January 14, 2005. Knowledge @ Wharton.
3. Joanna Barsh and Susie Cranston, *How Remarkable Women Lead* (New York, N.Y.: Crown Business, 2009).
4. Herminia Ibarra, Robin Ely, and Deborah Kolb, "Women Rising: The Unseen Barriers," *Harvard Business Review* (September 2013).
5. Claire Cain Miller, "For Incoming I.B.M. Chief, Self-Confidence Is Rewarded," *New York Times*, October 27, 2011.
6. Jessica Shambora, "Xerox's Next CEO, Ursula Burns," *Fortune*, May 22, 2009.
7. Anne Fisher, "Got a Mentor? Good. Now Find a Sponsor," *Fortune*, September 21, 2012.
8. Catalyst, "The Double-Bind Dilemma for Women in Leadership: Damned if You Do, Doomed if You Don't," July 2006.
9. Carly Fiorina, *Tough Choices: A Memoir* (New York, N.Y.: Penguin, 2006).
10. Batis M. Wiesenfeld, Naomi B. Wheller-Smith, and Sara L. Gallinsky, "Why Fair Bosses Fall Behind," *Harvard Business Review*, July 2011.
11. Mary Lou Décosterd, *How Women Are Transforming Leadership* (Santa Barbara, California: Praeger, 2013).
12. Indra Nooyi, "Adapting to Leading in a Changing World," Alessandro Benetton blog, July 25, 2012.www.allessandrobenettin.com.
13. Joanna Barsh and Susie Cranston, *How Remarkable Women Lead* (New York, N.Y: Crown Business, 2009).
14. Leading the Way: Ursula Burns. London Business School Interview conducted by Pearl Doherty, March 1, 2006.

CHAPTER 10

1. Jeffrey H. Dyer, Hal B. Gregersen, and Clayton M. Christensen, *The Innovator's DNA: Mastering the Five Skills of Disruptive Innovators* (Boston: Harvard Business School, 2011).
2. Burak Koyuncu, Shainaz Firfiray, Bjorn Claes, and Monika Hamori, "CEOs with a Functional Background in Operations: Reviewing Their Performance and Prevalence in the Top Post," *Human Resource Management* 49, no. 5 (September–October 2010).
3. Bill George, "America's Best Leaders: Anne Mulcahy, Xerox CEO," *US News and World Report*, November 19, 2008.
4. Ibid.
5. Bill George, Diana Mayer, and Andrew N., "Andrea Jung: Empowering Avon Women (A)," Harvard Business School, Case 9–404–035, January 28, 2008.
6. Fred Luthans, Carolyn M. Youssef, and Bruce Avolio, *Psychological Capital: Developing the Human Competitive Edge* (New York: Oxford University Press, 2006).
7. David l. Dotlich, Peter C. Cairo. *Why CEO's Fail.* (New York, NY.: Josey Bass, 2003).
8. Ibid.

INDEX